OXFORD WORLD'S CLASSICS

THE RENAISSANCE

WALTER PATER was born in Stepney in 1839 and educated at the King's School, Canterbury, and at Oxford, where he was subsequently elected a Fellow of Brasenose College. His career was one of quiet study and teaching, but his first book, *The Renaissance* (1873), caused something of a scandal both inside and outside the university because of its uncompromising advocacy of hedonism. Pater had acquired a reputation as a daring young aesthete, wit, and stylist and was seen as a formative influence on the Aesthetic Movement. He resigned his Fellowship to finish *Marius the Epicurean* (1885), one of the most celebrated and carefully wrought novels of the nineteenth century, and Pater's only novel. It was followed by a collection of short stories, *Imaginary Portraits* (1887), a collection of critical essays, *Appreciations* (1889), and the publication of the lectures on Plato that Pater gave at Oxford, *Plato and Platonism* (1893). Pater died in Oxford in 1894.

ADAM PHILLIPS is Principal Child Psychotherapist in the Wolverton Gardens Child and Family Consultation Centre (formerly Charing Cross Hospital). He has edited *Charles Lamb: Selected Prose* for Penguin and Edmund Burke's *A Philosophical Enquiry* for Oxford World's Classics. His study, *Winnicott*, is published in the Fontana Modern Masters series.

OXFORD WORLD'S CLASSICS

For over 100 years Oxford World's Classics have brought readers closer to the world's great literature. Now with over 700 titles—from the 4,000-year-old myths of Mesopotamia to the twentieth century's greatest novels—the series makes available lesser-known as well as celebrated writing.

The pocket-sized hardbacks of the early years contained introductions by Virginia Woolf, T. S. Eliot, Graham Greene, and other literary figures which enriched the experience of reading. Today the series is recognized for its fine scholarship and reliability in texts that span world literature, drama and poetry, religion, philosophy and politics. Each edition includes perceptive commentary and essential background information to meet the changing needs of readers.

OXFORD WORLD'S CLASSICS

===

WALTER PATER

The Renaissance
Studies in Art and Poetry

===

Edited with an Introduction and Notes by
ADAM PHILLIPS

OXFORD
UNIVERSITY PRESS

OXFORD
UNIVERSITY PRESS

Great Clarendon Street, Oxford OX2 6DP

Oxford University Press is a department of the University of Oxford.
It furthers the University's objective of excellence in research, scholarship,
and education by publishing worldwide in

Oxford New York

Athens Auckland Bangkok Bogotá Buenos Aires Calcutta
Cape Town Chennai Dar es Salaam Delhi Florence Hong Kong Istanbul
Karachi Kuala Lumpur Madrid Melbourne Mexico City Mumbai
Nairobi Paris São Paulo Singapore Taipei Tokyo Toronto Warsaw

with associated companies in Berlin Ibadan

Oxford is a registered trade mark of Oxford University Press
in the UK and in certain other countries

Published in the United States
by Oxford University Press Inc., New York

Introduction, Note on the Text, Select Bibliography,
Explanatory Notes © Adam Phillips 1986
Chronology © Ian Small 1985

The moral rights of the author have been asserted

Database right Oxford University Press (maker)

First published as a World's Classics paperback 1986
Reissued as an Oxford World's Classics paperback 1998

British Library Cataloguing in Publication Data

Data available

Library of Congress Cataloging in Publication Data
Pater, William, 1839–1894.
The Renaissance: studies in art and poetry.
(Oxford world's classics)
Bibliography: p.
1. Arts, Renaissance. I. Phillips, Adam.
II. Title.
[NX450.5.P37 1986] 700'.94 86–16414

ISBN–13: 978–0–19–283553–6
ISBN–10: 0–19–283553–X

8

Printed in Great Britain by
Clays Ltd, St Ives plc

CONTENTS

ACKNOWLEDGEMENTS

I would like to thank the following for their help: Geoffrey Summerfield, Hugh Haughton, and Geoffrey Weaver.

INTRODUCTION

I

One of the chief causes that can be assigned for the curiously commonplace character of most of the literature of our age is undoubtedly the decay of Lying as an art, a science, and a social pleasure.   Oscar Wilde, *The Decay of Lying*, 1891

The Renaissance now looks like what we have come to think of as a modernist text. It is densely self-referential: providing, intermittently, an implied commentary and critique of itself. It is also, through the endless qualifications of its elaborate style, drawing attention, sometimes obtrusively, to its own medium. It confuses intellectual categories by being at once a work of philosophy, fiction, cultural history, and aesthetic criticism. It even includes in its first two sentences a hint about how to read it. In short, *The Renaissance* was originally considered a misleading book. If it was seductive it was also, perhaps by the same token, inept. And yet in retrospect *The Renaissance* seems partly about what have been regarded as its flaws.

Though most of the reviews of the first edition of 1873 were favourable there was a prevailing unease that, as J. A. Symonds put it, 'the qualities of Mr Pater's temperament strongly modify his perceptions' (*Academy*, 15 March 1873). When Pater, with his pagan inclinations, wrote of Botticelli's madonnas that they, 'shrink from the pressure of the divine child, and plead in unmistakeable undertones for a warmer, lower humanity', Mrs Oliphant found him attributing sentiments that 'never entered into the most advanced imagination within two or three hundred years of Botticelli's time, and was as alien to the spirit of a medieval Italian, as it is perfectly consistent with that of a delicate Oxford don in the latter half of the nineteenth century' (*Blackwood's Magazine*, November 1873). The question was, what was Pater using his idea of the Renaissance for? Contemporary reviewers found the distinctively involved style of his impressionistic criticism either surprisingly convincing, or ludicrous, or both. It was not clear at the time whether Pater was inventive as a critic or merely negligent. To begin with, it was disarming to find paintings referred to in the text (as the Notes to this edition show) that Pater needlessly misattributed. As Sidney Colvin warned in his illuminating review, 'The book is not one for any beginner to turn to in search of "information"' (*Pall Mall Gazette*, March 1873).

In the very first essay of the book, 'Two Early French Stories', Pater had written of Abelard dying 'like Tannhäuser on his way to Rome', when we know that Pater knew from his source in Rémusat that the facts were at odds with his intended fiction. Abelard, as contemporary readers could have known, did not die as Pater wished. Not, it seems, a pilgrim whose eventual fate was undecided, he was actually absolved by the Pope, in all probability, before his death. His place in Pater's story depended on Pater 'modifying' the facts to make another kind of fiction possible. 'What might have happened had he reached his journey's end', he writes, 'is uncertain: and it is in this uncertain twilight that his relations to the general beliefs of his age has always remained.' In the uncertain twilight of Pater's scholarship cultural history became imaginative misrepresentation.

But when he used spurious texts, as he did occasionally in the essay on Michelangelo's poetry; or when, in the first two editions of the book, he footnoted the word 'kissing' in the essay on Winckelmann, 'Herman, Th.ii.c.ii.s21,(n.)16', was he not, perhaps, inciting the indignation of specialists, parodying the kind of scholarly apparatus that might normally have accompanied a book such as his? In a book explicitly interested both in historical method and the fortuities of error what was the significance of Pater's own mistakes, particularly those that looked deliberate? In an unpublished manuscript he had written of the 'elusive inscrutable mistakeable self'; 'mistakeable', then, as both easy to misrecognize, but also defined by the ability to make mistakes? Given his sense after reading Lessing and Hegel that, 'what seemed caprices or errors are ... seen to be [states] of development consequent upon each other with a sort of logical necessity', we should see at least some of Pater's inaccuracy in *The Renaissance* as idiosyncratic rather than unscrupulous, reflecting one of the dilemmas of the age.

In Pater's first published writing, his essay on Coleridge of 1866, he had suggested that: 'Modern thought is distinguished from ancient by its cultivation of the "relative" spirit in place of the "absolute" ... To the modern spirit nothing is, or can be rightly known, except relatively and under conditions' (*Westminster Review*, January 1866). The Christianity of Pater's Renaissance men is always being fortunately undermined by paganism, by the Hellenic ideal of harmonious perfection, by an enlightened sensuality. But the faith of his contemporaries in the truth of the Gospels had been dramatically eroded by Darwinism and the new historical approaches to the Bible. If there were no more stubborn facts; if nothing could now be proven to be absolutely and eternally true because life was now, by definition, change, what would it be to be rigorous? The risk now was of falling into what Wilde was to call 'careless habits of accuracy', of making thoughtless assumptions about what was true. It was these issues that *The Renaissance* was to highlight, and sometimes to caricature.

It is, for example, one of the characteristic ironies of *The Renaissance* that though Pater insists on the value of discriminating and refining his impressions, of accurately identifying them, his distinctive critical vocabulary is notably vague. The poet Edward Thomas, in his book on Pater, said that he was 'a man who has pondered the subject of the relation between things and words, and has come to no inspiring conclusion'. But it is part of Pater's subtlety to have exploited the invitation of inexact words. His indefinite words, 'sweet', 'peculiar', 'strange', 'delicate', are resonant as blanks that can evoke powerful personal associations in the reader. He is often evocative by being unspecific; and often, by the same token, close to self-parody. While the emphasis in *The Renaissance* was on precision, of impression and detail, the essays manifestly lacked a customary kind of rigour in matters of fact, that sometimes amounted to an absurd and characteristic disregard for the subjects.

'The information', Sidney Colvin wrote in his review, 'to be found in any one of the essays as to the personage who is his subject will be accurate as far as it goes, but will go only just far enough to carry the criticism, the definition of the impression the personage has made upon the writer individually. That, as Mr. Pater in his Preface leads us to expect, will be the main object of his essay.' Pater had made his intentions clear, and yet there was almost something irreverent about the way he fished for impressions, exploiting his subjects only for what they could evoke in him, at the same time drawing attention to the fact that this was what he was doing. It was noticeable that his biographical approach to his subjects was based on what could have been regarded as an over-identification with them, that tended to diminish their differences. Reading *The Renaissance* one cannot help but notice uncanny similarities between the lives, and even the deaths, of his subjects. But the task of aesthetic criticism, as Pater stated in the Preface, was to ask: 'What is this song or picture, this engaging personality in life, or in a book, to me? what effect does it really produce on me? . . . How is my nature modified by its presence, and under its influence?' The beguilingly simple questions Pater asks here, the questions that define his project, are neither esoteric, nor dogmatic. Nor are they exclusively concerned with art. They are the ordinary questions that initiate a sense of a self.

In his very earliest writing Pater had been preoccupied with the 'elusive inscrutable mistakeable self'. In *Diaphaneitè* (see Appendix) he had begun the description of a more passively receptive sensibility, an inwardness of response that was itself a new form of perception. It was an inverted kind of opportunism, allowing oneself to be worked on by experience, and being responsive to one's own emotional metabolism. One thing *The Renaissance* revealed was how coercive, how imaginatively coercive, such a sensibility could be. *The Renaissance* was seen by Pater's contemporaries to be the description of a temperament, and not any recognizable kind of cultural history at all. The title of the first edition, *Studies in the History of the Renaissance*, was changed in the second edition of 1877 to *The Renaissance; Studies in Art and*

Poetry. The original title, Pater's friend Mrs Mark Pattison wrote, was 'misleading; the historical element is precisely that which is wanting, and its absence marks the weak place of the whole book . . . the work is in no wise a contribution to the history of the Renaissance' (*Westminster Review*, April 1873). Pater had written about those artists, Leonardo, Michelangelo, Du Bellay, who were able in the most singular way to make themselves known through their art; he saw their lives, not their work alone, as representing the spirit of the age. But he would often call these lives 'legends' to draw attention to the invention that surrounded them, and made them in some way exemplary—turned them into history. So the history Pater wrote was often quite unrelated to actual lives; was, in fact, a kind of romance created by what he called 'half-imaginative memory'. It was almost as though for Pater, as Wilde wrote in 'The Decay of Lying', 'The only real people are the people who never existed.'

Mrs Mark Pattison also noted, in a wonderful image, the irony that though Pater stressed the need for a broad context of understanding, he had detached his subject 'wholly from its surroundings to suspend it isolated before him, as if it were indeed a kind of air-plant independent of ordinary sources of nourishment'. Pater had certainly found the Renaissance in several unexpected places: in France at the end of the twelfth and in the early thirteenth century, and as embodied by Winckelmann in the eighteenth century. 'By his enthusiasm for the things of the intellect and the imagination for their own sake,' he wrote of Winckelmann, 'by his Hellenism, his life-long struggle to attain to the Greek spirit, he is in sympathy with the humanists of a previous century.' The period was kept alive, Pater says, by Winckelmann's sympathetic identification with certain ideas; and implicitly by Pater's identification with Winckelmann. This was history as a series of influential recognitions, not history as chronology. Though Pater acknowledges that it is in Italy in the fifteenth century that 'the interest of the Renaissance mainly lies', he has redefined what he calls this 'outbreak of the human spirit' as being in evidence, in a sense, over six centuries.

Pater was critical in *The Renaissance*, and elsewhere in his writings, of what he called 'our exact modern formulas'; the kind of methodical approach or inflexible definition that might limit a study of the Renaissance to Italy in the fifteenth century. But while he suggests that definition itself imposes inappropriate constraints on a subject, in every essay of *The Renaissance* Pater makes definitive statements; about the period itself, about Hellenism, about humanism, about philosophy, about the 'true function' of the aesthetic critic. Even though he had written that all knowledge was now provisional, that there were no essential truths, there is a nostalgia in *The Renaissance* for the language of exact formulation—a language that would capture things: not necessarily the facts now, but what he was to call, in an important distinction, the 'soul-facts'; the only things that matter, as the pun suggests, but that may be of virtually private significance. For Pater the aim of any kind of artistic representation was to make these soul-facts shareable, and by doing so to reveal the soul of the artist.

Soul-facts were, by definition, in that ambiguous area between evidence and invention. The writing Pater was doing in *The Renassiance* involved him, inevitably, in these paradoxes of accuracy; the paradoxes Wilde was to celebrate in his book of essays of 1891, *Intentions*, that would provide the best introduction to the sophisticated ingenuousness of Pater's work. If *The Renaissance* was a work of art itself, and the critic an artist, then it was exempt, some reviewers suggested, from the kind of criticism reserved for other, more scholarly books. It was clear from the excessive revisions of the essays, and even from their unlikely order in the book, that *The Renaissance* had been carefully devised. Pater had dated each of the essays, so it was noticeable, for example, that the earliest essays were the last two in the book, 'Winckelmann' and the infamous Conclusion. And the Conclusion itself had been taken from an earlier review of William Morris's poems in the *Westminster Review* (October 1868). If the essays are read in the order of their composition the book is quite different. The Preface, for example, then appears to be an attempt to dilute some of the more desperate implications of the Conclusion. It was not, after all, Pater's ambiguous relationship to fact, his aesthetic criticism, that gave *The Renaissance* its initial notoriety. Pater, his friend Humphrey Ward wrote, 'was supposed to have a new and daring philosophy of his own and a wonderful gift of style, owing his fellowship (at Brasenose College) to these two, for he was no scholar as the Universities understand the word'.

The publication of *The Renaissance*, and in particular the Conclusion, was regarded as a scandal of moral negligence on Pater's part. 'Young men', A. C. Benson wrote in one of the early books on Pater, 'with vehement impulses, with no experience of the world, no idea of the solid and impenetrable weight of social traditions and prejudices, found in the principles enunciated by Pater with so much recondite beauty, so much magical charm, a new equation of values.' But it was possible that in *The Renaissance* Pater had announced what his near contemporary Nietzsche had called, the 'weightlessness' of modern men, the precariousness even of their prejudices. Pater's densely eclectic 'modern philosophy', with its epigraph from Heraclitus (also one of Nietzsche's idols), was preoccupied with how one could commit oneself to the absolute uncertainty of continuous change. Pater's so-called hedonism now seems more like an attempt to salvage something from the flux. The implausible assertion that 'To burn always with this hard, gem-like flame, to maintain this ecstasy, is success in life' was quoted more often than the devastating beginning of the sentence that follows it: 'In a sense it might even be said that our failure is to form habits'. His apparently hedonistic proposals concealed a terrible scepticism, a paralysing self-doubt about the 'elusive inscrutable mistakeable self'. 'Great passions', he wrote at the end of the Conclusion, 'may give us this quickened sense of life, ecstasy and sorrow of love, the various forms of enthusiastic activity, disinterested or otherwise, which come naturally to many of us. Only be sure it is passion—that it does yield you this fruit of a quickened, multiplied consciousness.' It was to be an accurate omen of what the self could simulate in the name of passion.

Mrs Humphrey Ward, the novelist, who was twenty-one when *The Renaissance* came out, claimed forty-five years later that she could remember 'very clearly', 'the effect of that book, and of the strange and poignant sense of beauty expressed in it; of its entire aloofness also from the Christian tradition of Oxford, its glorification of the higher and intenser forms of esthetic pleasure, of "passion" in the intellectual sense—as against the Christian doctrine of self-denial and renunciation. It was a doctrine that both stirred and scandalised Oxford. The bishop of the diocese thought it worthwhile to protest. There was a cry of neo-paganism, and various attempts at persecution' (*A Writer's Recollections*, 1918). But to appreciate now the broader impact of *The Renaissance* it must be seen in the context of Pater's influential predecessors, John Ruskin and Matthew Arnold, both of whom had been professors at Oxford, and whose lectures and writings had made possible Pater's new kind of cultural criticism.

II

They who made England, Italy or Greece venerable in the imagination, did so by sticking fast where they were, like an axis of the earth. Emerson, *Self-Reliance*, 1841

In 1865, at the age of twenty-six, Pater made his first journey to Italy, with his close friend Charles Shadwell to whom he eventually dedicated *The Renaissance*. They visited Ravenna, Pisa, and Florence where Pater was to see many of the works of art he was to write about on his return. As reproductions of works of art were relatively scarce at the time, many of the works Pater was to describe were not easily accessible. When Matthew Arnold wrote about Wordsworth, or, to a lesser extent, when Ruskin had written about Turner, the reader could, as it were, go back to the originals. When Pater wrote about Botticelli, and he was among the first to do so, his readers were entrusting themselves to his judgement. And criticism of the visual arts was itself a comparatively new genre in England. Reynolds and Hazlitt, to whom Pater pays little attention, had written extensively about painting; but it was Ruskin in the 1840s and 1850s who had written with a new kind of fervour and discrimination about the painting, sculpture, and architecture that were for him of crucial significance for the spiritual well-being of Britain in the mid-nineteenth century.

Pater had read Ruskin when he was nineteen, and though he never mentions him by name in *The Renaissance*, he is by implication a conspicuous presence in the book. In *The Stones of Venice* (1851, 1853) and *Modern Painters* (1843–60) Pater found Ruskin's moral distaste for the art of the Renaissance, and a passionate preference for the art of the High Middle Ages. Unlike Pater, Ruskin had located the Renaissance in Italy between the fourteenth and sixteenth century. Pater would also have found that much of *Modern Painters*, despite its title, was actually about the natural world, and Ruskin's commitment to a scrupulously accurate representation of nature; that for Ruskin the meticulous education of the eye was the way to a kind of moral authenticity; and that the powerful rhetoric of his art-criticism was in the service of his idiosyncratic Christianity. Those things that Ruskin, as the first great English critic of the visual arts, struggled to affirm, Pater, in his more tentative, insinuating style, would largely undermine.

Pater would put together an unusual group of subjects to represent the Renaissance, or rather, what he called 'the spirit of the Renaissance'. He would see the 'beauty' of the Renaissance wherever he found the paganism that for him was always waiting in the wings of Christianity. Where Ruskin had emphasized the artist's visual grasp, Pater would elaborate on the artist's internal world of moods and ideas; and by doing so would make vagueness, informed vagueness, intellectually respectable. Unlike Ruskin his aesthetic criticism would be neither prophetic nor technical; the self would be cultivated at leisure, not in strenuous social commitment. Criticism of the arts was to become, improbable as it seems, a refuge from the vested interests of a political world. In Pater's Renaissance there was no Machiavelli, and he wrote of Leonardo as he could have written about himself; 'No one had ever carried political indifferentism further.'

The Renaissance was, in part, an implicit critique of Ruskin;

both had emphasized the individual vision of the artist, but they had found it in different periods, and judged it by different standards. But Pater's 'political indifferentism' in *The Renaissance* had, in a sense, been sanctioned by Matthew Arnold. In his Inaugural Lecture at Oxford, 'The Function of Criticism at the Present Time' (1857), Arnold had said that 'English criticism' should be 'disinterested' by 'keeping aloof from practice ... by steadily refusing to lend itself to any of those ulterior, political, practical considerations about ideas, which plenty of people will be sure to attach to them'. The use of ideas should be deferred, he says, so they can make a better contribution, in the fullness of time, to society. Criticism for Arnold was a 'disinterested endeavour to learn and propagate the best that is known and thought in the world'. But in this famous lecture, to which Pater refers in *The Renaissance*, Arnold takes for granted the consensus of cultural values that are in question; he assumes that it is more or less self-evident what actually is the best that is known and thought, and that this can be established by the aim of criticism which is 'the endeavour ... to see the object as in itself it really is'. It is here that Pater takes issue with Arnold by pursuing the implications of his persuasive, but unargued conclusions.

' "To see the object as in itself it really is," has been justly said to be the aim of all true criticism whatever;', Pater writes in the Preface to *The Renaissance*, 'and in aesthetic criticism the first step towards seeing one's object as it really is, is to know one's impression as it really is, to discriminate it, to realise it distinctly.' Pater writes 'and' and not 'but' here in an attempt to assert the continuity of his work with Arnold's; a possible contradiction, as is usual with Pater, is made to look merely like an elaboration, because Pater's 'first step' towards knowing the object often looks like a step away. Once the critic begins to realize his impression the object might begin to disappear. 'She is older than the rocks among which she sits;' Pater writes of the Mona Lisa, 'like the vampire, she has been dead many times, and learned the secrets of the grave'. There is little in Pater's impression that enables the reader to recognize the painting, without having been told. *The Renaissance* revealed that Arnold's ideas of objectivity were more problematic than they at first seemed. Is the object as in itself it really is a consensus of personal impressions, or is such a consensus possible? What is it that makes a personal impression convincing, or even shareable? The notoriety of Pater's Mona Lisa could bear witness to some kind of shared recognitions. Impressions could not be disproved; at worst they could only be ridiculed. In fact the kind of contempt Pater's writing could evoke was in itself revealing, of aesthetic prejudice as well as principle. For Pater's admirers there were satisfactions but not proofs.

T. S. Eliot, in his influential essay of 1930, 'Arnold and Pater', dismissed Pater as 'the cultivated Oxford don and disciple of Arnold, for whom religion was a matter of feeling, and metaphysics not much more'. In Eliot's view Arnold had tried to replace religion with Culture, so Pater's writing was the inevitably decadent conclusion of such a tradition. 'The total effect', he wrote, 'of Arnold's philosophy is to set up Culture in the place of religion, and to leave religion to be laid waste by the anarchy of feeling. And Culture is a term which each man not only may interpret as he pleases, but must indeed interpret as he can. So the gospel of Pater follows naturally upon the prophecy of Arnold.' But the 'gospel of Pater' was actually to reveal Arnold's prophetic muddle. *The Rennaissance* was, implicitly, an exposure of Arnold's rhetoric of competent evaluation and willed cultural consensus, that in different terms Eliot was himself to inherit. Pater's impressionistic criticism threw the crucial issue of cultural consensus into disarray. While Pater's idea of culture in *The Renaissance* was manifestly rarified, his aesthetic criticism, with its few simple questions, acknowledged the inevitable pluralism of that culture. Everyone, after all, has impressions.

A reticent man, Pater continually tried to mute the outrageousness of the book he had written, and that had made him, for a short time, famous. But the excesses of the book, though elaborately understated, Wilde would recognize as the 'true spirit' of *The Renaissance*. Pater's always oblique, absurd humour in *The Renaissance*, for example, would turn into Wilde's parodies of earnestness. But *The Renaissance* turned into a stranger book than Pater had imagined.

NOTE ON THE TEXT

THIS edition of *The Renaissance* uses the text of the fourth edition of 1893, originally published by Macmillan and Co, London and New York. It was the final edition that Pater corrected. In the first edition of 1873 there were ten essays, five of which had appeared in periodicals as follows:

'Pico della Mirandola', *Fortnightly Review*, X, n.s., 1 October, 1871

'Sandro Botticelli', *Fortnightly Review*, VIII, n.s., August, 1870

'The Poetry of Michelangelo', *Fortnightly Review*, X, n.s., November, 1871

'Leonardo da Vinci', *Fortnightly Review*, VI, n.s., November, 1869

'Winckelmann', *Westminster Review*, XXXI, n.s., January, 1867.

'The School of Giorgione' was added in the third edition, having first been published in the *Fortnightly Review*, XIII, n.s., October, 1877. Pater revised almost every page of the republished essays. Unlike Donald L. Hill's superb edition (noted in the Select Bibliography) I have not corrected Pater's final text. Pater himself corrected and revised each of the four editions of *The Renaissance* published during his lifetime (1873, 1877, 1888, 1893).

SELECT BIBLIOGRAPHY

STUDY of *The Renaissance* now begins with Donald L. Hill's edition of the 1893 text, published by the University of California Press (1980). My edition, and my knowledge of Pater are heavily indebted to his work on *The Renaissance*, which is comprehensive and readable. *The Works of Walter Pater*, 10 vols. (London, 1910) are published by Macmillan; and the *Letters of Walter Pater* have been edited by Lawrence Evans (Oxford, 1970). Other than these the following are useful either about *The Renaissance*, or on matters relating to the book:

C. Baldick, *The Social Mission of English Criticism* (Oxford University Press, 1983)

A. C. Benson, *Pater. English Men of Letters*, 2nd edn. (London, 1926)

H. Bloom, *Selected Writings of Walter Pater*, edited with an introduction and notes by Harold Bloom (Columbia University Press, 1974)

G. Hough, *The Last Romantics* (Duckworth, 1949)

C. Ricks, *Walter Pater, Matthew Arnold, and Misquotation in The Force of Poetry* (Oxford University Press, 1985)

T. S. Eliot, *Arnold and Pater in The Eighteen-Eighties*, edited by Walter de la Mare for The Royal Society of Literature (1930)

Edward Thomas, *Walter Pater* (Martin Secker, 1913)

A CHRONOLOGY OF
WALTER PATER

1839 4 August: Pater born in Stepney.

1842 January: death of Pater's father.
Pater's mother, Maria Pater, moves to Enfield.

1853 Pater enrols at the King's School, Canterbury.

1854 25 February: Pater's mother dies.

1858 October: undergraduate at Queen's College, Oxford.

1862 BA in Literae Humaniores.

1864 Elected probationary Fellow at Brasenose College, Oxford.

1865 Summer: tours Italy with C. L. Shadwell, close friend and later his literary executor.

1866 January: 'Coleridge's Writings', Pater's first publication, appears anonymously in *Westminster Review*.

1867 Pater made lecturer at Brasenose.

1869 November: 'Notes On Leonardo da Vinci', Pater's first publication under his name, appears in the *Fortnightly Review*, Pater, Hester and Clara Pater move to Bradmore Road, Oxford.

1873 *Studies In The History Of The Renaissance* published.

1877 February: Pater announces his candidacy for the Oxford Professorship of Poetry. April: After a series of bitterly critical articles, Pater and later John Addington Symonds withdraw their candidacy. May: second edition of *The Renaissance* published.

1882 December: Pater, working on *Marius the Epicurean*, visits Rome.

1883 Pater resigns his Fellowship at Brasenose.

1885 March: *Marius the Epicurean* published. August: Walter, Clara, and Hester Pater move to 12 Earl's Terrace, Kensington. November: second edition of *Marius the Epicurean*.

1887 May: *Imaginary Portraits* published.

1889 November: *Appreciations* published.

1893 February: *Plato and Platonism* published. In the summer the Paters return to Oxford.

1894 30 July: Pater dies.

The Renaissance

DEDICATION

C. L. S.*

FEBRUARY, 1873.

CONTENTS

*Yet shall ye be as the wings of a dove**

PREFACE

MANY attempts have been made by writers on art and poetry to define beauty in the abstract, to express it in the most general terms, to find some universal formula for it. The value of these attempts has most often been in the suggestive and penetrating things said by the way. Such discussions help us very little to enjoy what has been well done in art or poetry, to discriminate between what is more and what is less excellent in them, or to use words like beauty, excellence, art, poetry, with a more precise meaning than they would otherwise have. Beauty, like all other qualities presented to human experience, is relative; and the definition of it becomes unmeaning and useless in proportion to its abstractness. To define beauty, not in the most abstract but in the most concrete terms possible, to find, not its universal formula, but the formula which expresses most adequately this or that special manifestation of it, is the aim of the true student of æsthetics.

'To see the object as in itself it really is,* has been justly said to be the aim of all true criticism whatever; and in æsthetic criticism the first step towards seeing one's object as it really is, is to know one's own impression as it really is, to discriminate it, to realise it distinctly. The objects with which æsthetic criticism deals—music, poetry, artistic and accomplished forms of human life—are indeed receptacles of so many powers or forces: they possess, like the products of nature, so many virtues or qualities. What is this song or picture, this engaging personality presented in life or in a book, to *me*? What effect does it really produce on me? Does it give me pleasure? and if so, what sort or degree of pleasure? How is my nature modified by its presence, and under its influence? The answers to these questions are the original facts with which the æsthetic critic has to do; and, as in the study of light, of morals, of number, one must realise such primary data for one's self, or not at all. And he who experiences these impressions strongly, and drives directly at the discrimination and analysis of them, has no need to trouble himself with the abstract question what beauty is in itself, or what its exact relation to truth or experience— metaphysical questions, as unprofitable as metaphysical questions elsewhere. He may pass them all by as being, answerable or not, of no interest to him.

The æsthetic critic, then, regards all the objects with which he has to do, all works of art, and the fairer forms of nature and human life, as powers or forces producing pleasurable sensations, each of a more or less peculiar or unique kind. This influence he feels, and wishes to explain, by analysing and reducing it to its elements. To him, the picture, the landscape, the engaging personality in life or in a book, *La Gioconda*, the hills of Carrara, Pico of Mirandola, are valuable for their virtues, as we say, in speaking of a herb, a wine, a gem; for the property each has of affecting one with a special, a unique, impression of pleasure. Our education becomes complete in proportion as our susceptibility to these impressions increases in depth and variety. And the function of the æsthetic critic is to distinguish, to analyse, and separate from its adjuncts, the virtue by which a picture, a landscape, a fair personality in life or in a book, produces this special impression of beauty or pleasure, to indicate what the source of that impression is, and under what conditions it is experienced. His end is reached when he has disengaged that virtue, and noted it, as a chemist notes some natural element, for himself and others; and the rule for those who would reach this end is stated with great exactness in the words of a recent critic of Sainte-Beuve:—*De se borner à connaître de près les belles choses, et à s'en nourrir en exquis amateurs, en humanistes accomplis.**

What is important, then, is not that the critic should possess a correct abstract definition of beauty for the intellect, but a certain kind of temperament, the power of being deeply moved by the presence of beautiful objects. He will remember always that beauty exists in many forms. To him all periods, types, schools of taste, are in themselves equal. In all ages there have been some excellent workmen, and some excellent work done. The question he asks is always:—In whom did the stir, the genius, the sentiment of the period find itself? where was the receptacle of its refinement, its elevation, its taste? 'The ages are all equal,' says William Blake, 'but genius is always above its age.'

Often it will require great nicety to disengage this virtue from the commoner elements with which it may be found in combination. Few artists, not Goethe or Byron even, work quite cleanly, casting off all *débris*, and leaving us only what the heat of their imagination has wholly fused and transformed. Take, for instance, the writings of Wordsworth. The heat of his genius, entering into the substance of his work, has crystallised a part, but only a part, of it; and in that great mass of verse there is much which might well be forgotten. But scattered up and down it, sometimes fusing and transforming entire compositions, like the Stanzas on *Resolution and Independence*, or the *Ode on the Recollections of Childhood*, sometimes, as if at random, depositing a fine crystal here or there, in a matter it does not wholly search through and transmute, we trace the action of his unique, incommunicable faculty, that strange, mystical sense of a life in natural things, and of man's life as a part of nature, drawing strength and colour and character from local influences, from the hills and streams, and from natural sights and sounds. Well! that is the *virtue*, the active principle in Wordsworth's poetry; and then the function of the critic of Wordsworth is to follow up that active principle, to disengage it, to mark the degree in which it penetrates his verse.

The subjects of the following studies are taken from the history of the *Renaissance*, and touch what I think the chief points in that complex, many-sided movement. I have explained in the first of them what I understand by the word, giving it a much wider scope than was intended by those who originally used it to denote that revival of classical antiquity in the fifteenth century which was only one of many results of a general excitement and enlightening of the human mind, but of which the great aim and achievements of what, as Christian art, is often falsely opposed to the

Renaissance, were another result. This outbreak of the
human spirit may be traced far into the middle age itself,
with its motives already clearly pronounced, the care for
physical beauty, the worship of the body, the breaking down
of those limits which the religious system of the middle age
imposed on the heart and the imagination. I have taken as
an example of this movement, this earlier Renaissance
within the middle age itself, and as an expression of its
qualities, two little compositions in early French; not because
they constitute the best possible expression of them, but
because they help the unity of my series, inasmuch as the
Renaissance ends also in France, in French poetry, in a phase
of which the writings of Joachim du Bellay are in many ways
the most perfect illustration. The Renaissance, in truth, put
forth in France an aftermath, a wonderful later growth, the
products of which have to the full that subtle and delicate
sweetness which belongs to a refined and comely decadence,
as its earliest phases have the freshness which belongs to all
periods of growth in art, the charm of *ascêsis*, of the austere
and serious girding of the loins in youth.

But it is in Italy, in the fifteenth century, that the interest
of the Renaissance mainly lies,—in that solemn fifteenth
century which can hardly be studied too much, not merely
for its positive results in the things of the intellect and the
imagination, its concrete works of art, its special and prominent personalities, with their profound æsthetic charm, but
for its general spirit and character, for the ethical qualities of
which it is a consummate type.

The various forms of intellectual activity which together
make up the culture of an age, move for the most part from
different starting-points, and by unconnected roads. As
products of the same generation they partake indeed of a
common character, and unconsciously illustrate each other;
but of the producers themselves, each group is solitary,
gaining what advantage or disadvantage there may be in
intellectual isolation. Art and poetry, philosophy and the
religious life, and that other life of refined pleasure and
action in the conspicuous places of the world, are each of
them confined to its own circle of ideas, and those who

prosecute either of them are generally little curious of the thoughts of others. There come, however, from time to time, eras of more favourable conditions, in which the thoughts of men draw nearer together than is their wont, and the many interests of the intellectual world combine in one complete type of general culture. The fifteenth century in Italy is one of these happier eras, and what is sometimes said of the age of Pericles* is true of that of Lorenzo*:—it is an age productive in personalities, many-sided, centralised, complete. Here, artists and philosophers and those whom the action of the world has elevated and made keen, do not live in isolation, but breathe a common air, and catch light and heat from each other's thoughts. There is a spirit of general elevation and enlightenment in which all alike communicate. The unity of this spirit gives unity to all the various products of the Renaissance; and it is to this intimate alliance with mind, this participation in the best thoughts which that age produced, that the art of Italy in the fifteenth century owes much of its grave dignity and influence.

I have added an essay on Winckelmann, as not incongruous with the studies which precede it, because Winckelmann, coming in the eighteenth century, really belongs in spirit to an earlier age. By his enthusiasm for the things of the intellect and the imagination for their own sake, by his Hellenism, his life-long struggle to attain to the Greek spirit, he is in sympathy with the humanists of a previous century. He is the last fruit of the Renaissance, and explains in a striking way its motive and tendencies.

1873.

TWO EARLY FRENCH STORIES

The history of the Renaissance ends in France, and carries us away from Italy to the beautiful cities of the country of the Loire. But it was in France also, in a very important sense, that the Renaissance had begun. French writers, who are fond of connecting the creations of Italian genius with a French origin, who tell us how Saint Francis of Assisi took not his name only, but all those notions of chivalry and romantic love which so deeply penetrated his thoughts, from a French source, how Boccaccio* borrowed the outlines of his stories from the old French *fabliaux*, and how Dante himself expressly connects the origin of the art of miniature-painting with the city of Paris,* have often dwelt on this notion of a Renaissance in the end of the twelfth and the beginning of the thirteenth century, a Renaissance within the limits of the middle age itself—a brilliant, but in part abortive effort to do for human life and the human mind what was afterwards done in the fifteenth. The word *Renaissance*, indeed, is now generally used to denote not merely the revival of classical antiquity which took place in the fifteenth century, and to which the word was first applied, but a whole complex movement, of which that revival of classical antiquity was but one element or symptom. For us the Renaissance is the name of a many-sided but yet united movement, in which the love of the things of the intellect and the imagination for their own sake, the desire for a more liberal and comely way of conceiving life, make themselves felt, urging those who experience this desire to search out first one and then another means of intellectual or imaginative enjoyment, and directing them not only to the discovery of old and forgotten sources of this enjoyment, but to the divination of fresh sources thereof—new experiences, new subjects of poetry, new forms of art. Of such feeling there was a great outbreak in the end of the twelfth and the beginning of the following century. Here and there, under rare and happy conditions, in pointed architecture, in the doctrines of romantic love, in the poetry of Provence, the rude strength of the middle age turns to sweetness; and the taste for sweetness generated there becomes the seed of the classical revival in it, prompting it constantly to seek after the springs of perfect sweetness in the Hellenic world. And coming after a long period in which this instinct had been crushed, that true 'dark age,' in which so many sources of intellectual and imaginative enjoyment had actually disappeared, this outbreak is rightly called a Renaissance, a revival.

Theories which bring into connexion with each other modes of thought and feeling, periods of taste, forms of art and poetry, which the narrowness of men's minds constantly tends to oppose to each other, have a great stimulus for the intellect, and are almost always worth understanding. It is so with this theory of a Renaissance within the middle age, which seeks to establish a continuity between the most characteristic work of that period, the sculpture of Chartres, the windows of Le Mans, and the work of the later Renaissance, the work of Jean Cousin and Germain Pilon,* thus healing that rupture between the middle age and the Renaissance which has so often been exaggerated. But it is not so much the ecclesiastical art of the middle age, its sculpture and painting—work certainly done in a great measure for pleasure's sake, in which even a secular, a rebellious spirit often betrays itself—but rather its profane poetry, the poetry of Provence, and the magnificent after-growth of that poetry in Italy and France, which those French writers have in view when they speak of this medieval Renaissance. In that poetry, earthly passion, with its intimacy, its freedom, its variety—the liberty of the heart—makes itself felt; and the name of Abelard, the great scholar and the great lover, connects the expression of this liberty of heart with the free play of human intelligence around all subjects presented to it, with the liberty of the intellect, as that age understood it.

Every one knows the legend of Abelard;* a legend hardly less passionate, certainly not less characteristic of the middle age, than the legend of Tannhäuser; how the famous and comely clerk, in whom Wisdom herself, self-possessed, pleasant, and discreet, seemed to sit enthroned, came to live in the house of a canon of the church of *Notre-Dame*, where dwelt a girl, Heloïse, believed to be the old priest's orphan niece; how the old priest had testified his love for her by giving her an education then unrivalled, so that rumour asserted that, through the knowledge of languages, enabling her to penetrate into the mysteries of the older world, she had become a sorceress, like the Celtic druidesses; and how as Abelard and Heloïse sat together at home there, to refine a little further on the nature of abstract ideas, 'Love made himself of the party with them.' You conceive the temptations of the scholar, who, in such dreamy tranquillity, amid the bright and busy spectacle of the 'Island,' lived in a world of something like shadows; and that for one who knew so well how to assign its exact value to every abstract thought, those restraints which lie on the consciences of other men had been relaxed. It appears that he composed many verses in the vulgar tongue: already the young men sang them on the quay below the house. Those songs, says M. de Rémusat,* were probably in the taste of the *Trouvères*, 'of whom he was one of the first in date, or, so to speak, the predecessor.' It is the same spirit which has moulded the famous 'letters,' written in the quaint Latin of the middle age.

At the foot of that early Gothic tower, which the next generation raised to grace the precincts of Abelard's school, on the 'Mountain of Saint Geneviève,' the historian Michelet* sees in thought 'a terrible assembly; not the hearers of Abelard alone, fifty bishops, twenty cardinals, two popes, the whole body of scholastic philosophy; not only the learned Heloïse, the teaching of languages, and the Renaissance; but Arnold of Brescia*—that is to say, the revolution.' And so from the rooms of this shadowy house by the Seine side we see that spirit going abroad, with its qualities already well defined, its intimacy, its languid sweetness, its rebellion, its subtle skill in dividing the elements of human passion, its care for physical beauty, its worship of the body, which penetrated the early literature of Italy, and finds an echo even in Dante.

That Abelard is not mentioned in the *Divine Comedy* may

appear a singular omission to the reader of Dante, who seems
to have inwoven into the texture of his work whatever had
impressed him as either effective in colour or spiritually
significant among the recorded incidents of actual life.
Nowhere in his great poem do we find the name, nor so much
as an allusion to the story of one who had left so deep a mark
on the philosophy of which Dante was an eager student, of
whom in the *Latin Quarter*, and from the lips of scholar or
teacher in the University of Paris, during his sojourn among
them, he can hardly have failed to hear. We can only
suppose that he had indeed considered the story and the
man, and abstained from passing judgment as to his place in
the scheme of 'eternal justice.'

In the famous legend of Tannhäuser, the erring knight
makes his way to Rome, to seek absolution at the centre of
Christian religion. 'So soon,' thought and said the Pope, 'as
the staff in his hand should bud and blossom, so soon might
the soul of Tannhäuser be saved, and no sooner;' and it came
to pass not long after that the dry wood of a staff which the
Pope had carried in his hand was covered with leaves and
flowers. So, in the cloister of Godstow, a petrified tree was
shown of which the nuns told that the fair Rosamond,* who
had died among them, had declared that, the tree being then
alive and green, it would be changed into stone at the hour
of her salvation. When Abelard died, like Tannhäuser, he
was on his way to Rome. What might have happened had he
reached his journey's end is uncertain; and it is in this
uncertain twilight that his relation to the general beliefs of
his age has always remained. In this, as in other things, he
prefigures the character of the Renaissance, that movement
in which, in various ways, the human mind wins for itself a
new kingdom of feeling and sensation and thought, not
opposed to but only beyond and independent of the spiritual
system then actually realised. The opposition into which
Abelard is thrown, which gives its colour to his career, which
breaks his soul to pieces, is a no less subtle opposition than
that between the merely professional, official, hireling ministers of that system, with their ignorant worship of system for

its own sake, and the true child of light, the humanist, with reason and heart and senses quick, while theirs were almost dead. He reaches out towards, he attains, modes of ideal living, beyond the prescribed limits of that system, though in essential germ, it may be, contained within it. As always happens, the adherents of the poorer and narrower culture had no sympathy with, because no understanding of, a culture richer and more ample than their own. After the discovery of wheat they would still live upon acorns—*après l'invention du blé ils voulaient encore vivre du gland*;* and would hear of no service to the higher needs of humanity with instruments not of their forging.

But the human spirit, bold through those needs, was too strong for them. Abelard and Heloïse write their letters— letters with a wonderful outpouring of soul—in medieval Latin; and Abelard, though he composes songs in the vulgar tongue, writes also in Latin those treatises in which he tries to find a ground of reality below the abstractions of philosophy, as one bent on trying all things by their congruity with human experience, who had felt the hand of Heloïse, and looked into her eyes, and tested the resources of humanity in her great and energetic nature. Yet it is only a little later, early in the thirteenth century, that French prose romance begins; and in one of the pretty volumes of the *Bibliothèque Elzevirienne** some of the most striking fragments of it may be found, edited with much intelligence. In one of these thirteenth-century stories, *Li Amitiez de Ami et Amile*, that free play of human affection, of the claims of which Abelard's story is an assertion, makes itself felt in the incidents of a great friendship, a friendship pure and generous, pushed to a sort of passionate exaltation, and more than faithful unto death. Such comradeship, though instances of it are to be found everywhere, is still especially a classical motive; Chaucer expressing the sentiment of it so strongly in an antique tale, that one knows not whether the love of both Palamon and Arcite for Emelya, or of those two for each other, is the chiefer subject of the *Knight's Tale*—

He cast his eyen upon Emelya,
And therewithal he bleynte and cried, ah!
As that he stongen were unto the herte.

What reader does not refer something of the bitterness of that cry to the spoiling, already foreseen, of the fair friendship, which had made the prison of the two lads sweet hitherto with its daily offices?

The friendship of Amis and Amile is deepened by the romantic circumstance of an entire personal resemblance between the two heroes, through which they pass for each other again and again, and thereby into many strange adventures; that curious interest of the *Doppelgänger*,* which begins among the stars with the Dioscuri,* being entwined in and out through all the incidents of the story, like an outward token of the inward similitude of their souls. With this, again, is connected, like a second reflexion of that inward similitude, the conceit of two marvellously beautiful cups, also exactly like each other—children's cups, of wood, but adorned with gold and precious stones. These two cups, which by their resemblance help to bring the friends together at critical moments, were given to them by the Pope, when he baptised them at Rome, whither the parents had taken them for that purpose, in gratitude for their birth. They cross and recross very strangely in the narrative, serving the two heroes almost like living things, and with that well-known effect of a beautiful object, kept constantly before the eye in a story or poem, of keeping sensation well awake, and giving a certain air of refinement to all the scenes into which it enters. That sense of fate, which hangs so much of the shaping of human life on trivial objects, like Othello's strawberry handkerchief, is thereby heightened, while witness is borne to the enjoyment of beautiful handiwork by a primitive people, their simple wonder at it, so that they give it an oddly significant place among the factors of a human history.

Amis and Amile, then, are true to their comradeship through all trials; and in the end it comes to pass that at a moment of great need Amis takes the place of Amile in a tournament for life or death. 'After this it happened that a leprosy fell upon Amis, so that his wife would not approach him, and wrought to strangle him. He departed therefore from his home, and at last prayed his servants to carry him to the house of Amile;' and it is in what follows that the curious strength of the piece shows itself:—

'His servants, willing to do as he desired, carried him to the place where Amile was; and they began to sound their rattles before the court of Amile's house, as lepers are accustomed to do. And when Amile heard the noise he commanded one of his servants to carry meat and bread to the sick man, and the cup which was given to him at Rome filled with good wine. And when the servant had done as he was commanded, he returned and said, Sir, if I had not thy cup in my hand, I should believe that the cup which the sick man has was thine, for they are alike, the one to the other, in height and fashion. And Amile said, Go quickly and bring him to me. And when Amis stood before his comrade Amile demanded of him who he was, and how he had gotten that cup. I am of Briquain le Chastel, answered Amis, and the cup was given to me by the Bishop of Rome, who baptised me. And when Amile heard that, he knew that it was his comrade Amis, who had delivered him from death, and won for him the daughter of the King of France to be his wife. And straightway he fell upon him, and began weeping greatly, and kissed him. And when his wife heard that, she ran out with her hair in disarray, weeping and distressed exceedingly, for she remembered that it was he who had slain the false Ardres. And thereupon they placed him in a fair bed, and said to him, Abide with us until God's will be accomplished in thee, for all we have is at thy service. So he and the two servants abode with them.

'And it came to pass one night, when Amis and Amile lay in one chamber without other companions, that God sent His angel Raphael to Amis, who said to him, Amis, art thou asleep? And he, supposing that Amile had called him, answered and said, I am not asleep, fair comrade! And the angel said to him, Thou hast answered well, for thou art the comrade of the heavenly citizens.—I am Raphael, the angel of our Lord, and am come to tell thee how thou mayest be healed; for thy prayers are heard. Thou shalt bid Amile, thy comrade, that he slay his two children and wash thee in their blood, and so thy body shall be made whole. And Amis said to him, Let not this thing be, that my comrade should become a murderer for my sake. But the angel said, It is convenient that he do this. And thereupon the angel departed.

'And Amile also, as if in sleep, heard those words; and he awoke and said, Who is it, my comrade, that hath spoken with thee? And Amis answered, No man; only I have prayed to our Lord, as I am accustomed. And Amile said, Not so! but some one hath spoken with thee. Then he arose and went to the door of the chamber; and finding it shut he said, Tell me, my brother, who it was said those words to thee to-night. And Amis began to weep greatly, and told him that it was Raphael, the angel of the Lord, who had said to him, Amis, our Lord commands thee that thou bid Amile slay his two children, and wash thee in their blood, and so thou shalt be healed of thy leprosy. And Amile was greatly disturbed at those words, and said, I would have given to thee my man-servants and my maid-servants and all my goods, and thou feignest that an angel hath spoken to thee that I should slay my two children. And immediately Amis began to weep, and said, I know that I have spoken to thee a terrible thing, but constrained thereto; I pray thee cast me not away from the shelter of thy house. And Amile answered that what he had covenanted with him, that he would perform, unto the hour of his death: But I conjure thee, said he, by the faith which there is between me and thee, and by our comradeship, and by the baptism we received together at Rome, that thou tell me whether it was man or angel said that to thee. And Amis answered again, So truly as an angel hath spoken to me this night, so may God deliver me from my infirmity!

'Then Amile began to weep in secret, and thought within himself: If this man was ready to die before the king for me, shall I not for him slay my children? Shall I not keep faith with him who was faithful to me even unto death? And Amile tarried no longer, but departed to the chamber of his wife, and bade her go hear the Sacred Office. And he took a sword, and went to the bed where the children were lying, and found them asleep. And he lay down over them and began to weep bitterly and said, Hath any man yet heard of a father who of his own will slew his children? Alas, my children! I am no longer your father, but your cruel murderer.

'And the children awoke at the tears of their father, which fell upon them; and they looked up into his face and began to laugh. And as they were of the age of about three years, he said, Your laughing will be turned into tears, for your innocent blood must now be shed, and therewith he cut off their heads. Then he laid them back in the bed, and put the heads upon the bodies, and covered them as though they slept: and with the blood which he had taken he washed his comrade, and said, Lord Jesus Christ! who hast commanded men to keep faith on earth, and didst heal the leper by Thy word! cleanse now my comrade, for whose love I have shed the blood of my children.

'Then Amis was cleansed of his leprosy. And Amile clothed his companion in his best robes; and as they went to the church to give thanks, the bells, by the will of God, rang of their own accord. And when the people of the city heard that, they ran together to see the marvel. And the wife of Amile, when he saw Amis and Amile coming, asked which of the twain was her husband, and said, I know well the vesture of them both, but I know not which of them is Amile. And Amile said to her, I am Amile, and my companion is Amis, who is healed of his sickness. And she was full of wonder, and desired to know in what manner he was healed. Give thanks to our Lord, answered Amile, but trouble not thyself as to the manner of the healing.

'Now neither the father nor the mother had yet entered where the children were; but the father sighed heavily, because they were dead, and the mother asked for them, that they might rejoice together; but Amile said, Dame! let the children sleep. And it was already the hour of Tierce. And going in alone to the children to weep over them, he found them at play in the bed; only, in the place of the sword-cuts about their throats was as it were a thread of crimson. And he took them in his arms and carried them to his wife and said, Rejoice greatly, for thy children whom I had slain by the commandment of the angel are alive, and by their blood is Amis healed.'

There, as I said, is the strength of the old French story. For the Renaissance has not only the sweetness which it derives from the classical world, but also that curious strength of which there are great resources in the true middle age. And as I have illustrated the early strength of the Renaissance by the story of Amis and Amile, a story which comes from the North, in which a certain racy Teutonic flavour is perceptible, so I shall illustrate that other element, its early sweetness, a languid excess of sweetness even, by another story printed in the same volume of the *Bibliothèque Elzevirienne*, and of about the same date, a story which comes, characteristically, from the South, and connects itself with the literature of Provence.

The central love-poetry of Provence, the poetry of the *Tenson* and the *Aubade*,* of Bernard de Ventadour and Pierre Vidal,* is poetry for the few, for the elect and peculiar people of the kingdom of sentiment. But below this intenser poetry there was probably a wide range of literature, less serious and elevated, reaching, by lightness of form and comparative homeliness of interest, an audience which the concentrated passion of those higher lyrics left untouched. This literature has long since perished, or lives only in later French or Italian versions. One such version, the only representative of its species, M. Fauriel* thought he detected in the story of *Aucassin and Nicolette*, written in the French of the latter half of the thirteenth century, and preserved in a unique manuscript, in the national library of Paris; and there were reasons which made him divine for it a still more ancient ancestry, traces in it of an Arabian origin, as in a leaf lost out of some early *Arabian Nights*[1].

The little book loses none of its interest through the criticism which finds in it only a traditional subject, handed on by one people to another; for after passing thus from hand to hand, its outline is still clear, its surface untarnished; and, like many other stories, books, literary and artistic conceptions of the middle age, it has come to have in this way a sort of personal history, almost as full of risk and adventure as that of its own heroes. The writer himself calls the piece a *cantefable*, a tale told in prose, but with its incidents and sentiment helped forward by songs, inserted at irregular intervals. In the junctions of the story itself there are signs of roughness and want of skill, which make one suspect that the prose was only put together to connect a series of songs—a series of songs so moving and attractive that people wished to heighten and dignify their effect by a regular framework of setting. Yet the songs themselves are of the simplest kind, not rhymed even, but only imperfectly assonant, stanzas of twenty or thirty lines apiece, all ending with a similar vowel sound. And here, as elsewhere in that early poetry, much of the interest lies in the spectacle of the formation of a new artistic sense. A novel art is arising, the music of rhymed poetry, and in the songs of Aucassin and Nicolette, which seem always on the point of passing into true rhyme, but which halt somehow, and can never quite take flight, you see people just growing aware of the elements of a new music in their possession, and anticipating how pleasant such music might become.

The piece was probably intended to be recited by a company of trained performers, many of whom, at least for the lesser parts, were probably children. The songs are

---

[1] Recently, *Aucassin and Nicolette* has been edited and translated into English, with much graceful scholarship, by Mr. F. W. Bourdillon. Still more recently we have had a translation—a poet's translation—from the ingenious and versatile pen of Mr. Andrew Lang. The reader should consult also the chapter on 'The Outdoor Poetry,' in Vernon Lee's most interesting *Euphorion; being Studies of the Antique and Mediaeval in the Renaissance*, a work abounding in knowledge and insight on the subjects of which it treats.

introduced by the rubric, *Or se cante* (*ici on chante*) and each
division of prose by the rubric, *Or dient et content et fabloient* (*ici
on conte*). The musical notes of a portion of the songs have
been preserved; and some of the details are so descriptive
that they suggested to M. Fauriel the notion that the words
had been accompanied throughout by dramatic action. That
mixture of simplicity and refinement which he was surprised
to find in a composition of the thirteenth century, is shown
sometimes in the turn given to some passing expression or
remark; thus 'the Count de Garins was old and frail, his time
was over'—*Li quens Garins de Beaucaire estoit vix et frales; si avoit
son tans trespassè*. And then all is so realised! One sees the
ancient forest, with its disused roads grown deep with grass,
and the place where seven roads meet—*u a forkeut set cemin qui
s'en vont par le païs*; we hear the light-hearted country-people
calling each other by their rustic names, and putting forward, as their spokesman, one among them who is more
eloquent and ready than the rest—*li un qui plus fu enparlés des
autres*; for the little book has its burlesque element also, so
that one hears the faint, far-off laughter still. Rough as it is,
the piece certainly possesses this high quality of poetry, that
it aims at a purely artistic effect. Its subject is a great sorrow,
yet it claims to be a thing of joy and refreshment, to be
entertained not for its matter only, but chiefly for its
manner; it is *cortois*, it tells us, *et bien assis*.*

For the student of manners, and of the old French
language and literature, it has much interest of a purely
antiquarian order. To say of an ancient literary composition
that it has an antiquarian interest, often means that it has no
distinct æsthetic interest for the reader of to-day. Antiquarianism, by a purely historical effort, by putting its object in
perspective, and setting the reader in a certain point of view,
from which what gave pleasure to the past is pleasurable for
him also, may often add greatly to the charm we receive
from ancient literature. But the first condition of such aid
must be a real, direct, æsthetic charm in the thing itself.
Unless it has that charm, unless some purely artistic quality
went to its original making, no merely antiquarian effort can
ever give it an æsthetic value, or make it a proper subject of

æsthetic criticism. This quality, wherever it exists, it is always pleasant to define, and discriminate from the sort of borrowed interest which an old play, or an old story, may very likely acquire through a true antiquarianism. The story of Aucassin and Nicolette has something of this quality. Aucassin, the only son of Count Garins of Beaucaire, is passionately in love with Nicolette, a beautiful girl of unknown parentage, bought of the Saracens, whom his father will not permit him to marry. The story turns on the adventures of these two lovers, until at the end of the piece their mutual fidelity is rewarded. These adventures are of the simplest sort, adventures which seem to be chosen for the happy occasion they afford of keeping the eye of the fancy, perhaps the outward eye, fixed on pleasant objects, a garden, a ruined tower, the little hut of flowers which Nicolette constructs in the forest whither she escapes from her enemies, as a token to Aucassin that she has passed that way. All the charm of the piece is in its details, in a turn of peculiar lightness and grace given to the situations and traits of sentiment, especially in its quaint fragments of early French prose.

All through it one feels the influence of that faint air of overwrought delicacy, almost of wantonness, which was so strong a characteristic of the poetry of the Troubadours. The Troubadours themselves were often men of great rank; they wrote for an exclusive audience, people of much leisure and great refinement, and they came to value a type of personal beauty which has in it but little of the influence of the open air and sunshine. There is a languid Eastern deliciousness in the very scenery of the story, the full-blown roses, the chamber painted in some mysterious manner where Nicolette is imprisoned, the cool brown marble, the almost nameless colours, the odour of plucked grass and flowers. Nicolette herself well becomes this scenery, and is the best illustration of the quality I mean—the beautiful, weird, foreign girl, whom the shepherds take for a fay, who has the knowledge of simples, the healing and beautifying qualities of leaves and flowers, whose skilful touch heals Aucassin's sprained shoulder, so that he suddenly leaps from the ground; the mere sight of whose white flesh, as she passed the place where he lay, healed a pilgrim stricken with sore disease, so that he rose up, and returned to his own country. With this girl Aucassin is so deeply in love that he forgets all knightly duties. At last Nicolette is shut up to get her out of his way, and perhaps the prettiest passage in the whole piece is the fragment of prose which describes her escape:—

'Aucassin was put in prison, as you have heard, and Nicolette remained shut up in her chamber. It was summer-time, in the month of May, when the days are warm and long and clear, and the nights coy and serene.

'One night Nicolette, lying on her bed, saw the moon shine clear through the little window, and heard the nightingale sing in the garden, and then came the memory of Aucassin, whom she so much loved. She thought of the Count Garins of Beaucaire, who mortally hated her, and, to be rid of her, might at any moment cause her to be burned or drowned. She perceived that the old woman who kept her company was asleep; she rose and put on the fairest gown she had; she took the bed-clothes and the towels, and knotted them together like a cord, as far as they would go. Then she tied the end to a pillar of the window, and let herself slip down quite softly into the garden, and passed straight across it, to reach the town.

'Her hair was yellow in small curls, her smiling eyes blue-green, her face clear and feat, the little lips very red, the teeth small and white; and the daisies which she crushed in passing, holding her skirt high behind and before, looked dark against her feet; the girl was so white!

'She came to the garden-gate and opened it, and walked through the streets of Beaucaire, keeping on the dark side of the way to be out of the light of the moon, which shone quietly in the sky. She walked as fast as she could, until she came to the tower where Aucassin was. The tower was set about with pillars, here and there. She pressed herself against one of the pillars, wrapped herself closely in her mantle, and putting her face to a chink of the tower, which was old and ruined, she heard Aucassin crying bitterly within, and when she had listened awhile she began to speak.'—

But scattered up and down through this lighter matter, always tinged with humour and often passing into burlesque, which makes up the general substance of the piece, there are morsels of a different quality, touches of some intenser sentiment, coming it would seem from the profound and energetic spirit of the Provençal poetry itself, to which the inspiration of the book has been referred. Let me gather up these morsels of deeper colour, these expressions of the ideal intensity of love, the motive which really unites together the fragments of the little composition. Dante, the perfect flower of ideal love, has recorded how the tyranny of that 'Lord of terrible aspect'* became actually physical, blinding his senses, and suspending his bodily forces. In this, Dante is but the central expression and type of experiences known well enough to the initiated, in that passionate age. Aucassin represents this ideal intensity of passion—

> *Aucassin, li biax, li blons,*
> *Li gentix, li amorous;—*

slim, tall, debonair, *dansellon*, as the singers call him, with his curled yellow hair, and eyes of *vair*, who faints with love, as Dante fainted, who rides all day through the forest in search of Nicolette, while the thorns tear his flesh, so that one might have traced him by the blood upon the grass, and who weeps at eventide because he has not found her, who has the malady of his love, and neglects all knightly duties. Once he is induced to put himself at the head of his people, that they, seeing him before them, might have more heart to defend themselves; then a song relates how the sweet, grave figure goes forth to battle, in dainty, tight-laced armour. It is the very image of the Provençal love-god, no longer a child, but grown to pensive youth, as Pierre Vidal met him, riding on a white horse, fair as the morning, his vestment embroidered with flowers. He rode on through the gates into the open plain beyond. But as he went, that great malady of his love came upon him. The bridle fell from his hands; and like one who sleeps walking, he was carried on into the midst of his enemies, and heard them talking together how they might most conveniently kill him.

One of the strongest characteristics of that outbreak of the reason and the imagination, of that assertion of the liberty of the heart, in the middle age, which I have termed a medieval Renaissance, was its antinomianism, its spirit of rebellion and revolt against the moral and religious ideas of the time. In their search after the pleasures of the senses and the imagination, in their care for beauty, in their worship of the body, people were impelled beyond the bounds of the Christian ideal; and their love became sometimes a strange idolatry, a strange rival religion. It was the return of that ancient Venus, not dead, but only hidden for a time in the caves of the Venusberg, of those old pagan gods still going to and fro on the earth, under all sorts of disguises. And this element in the middle age, for the most part ignored by those writers who have treated it pre-eminently as the 'Age of Faith'—this rebellious and antinomian element, the recognition of which has made the delineation of the middle age by the writers of the Romantic school in France, by Victor Hugo for instance in *Notre-Dame de Paris*,* so suggestive and exciting—is found alike in the history of Abelard and the legend of Tannhäuser. More and more, as we come to mark changes and distinctions of temper in what is often in one all-embracing confusion called the middle age, that rebellion, that sinister claim for liberty of heart and thought, comes to the surface. The Albigensian movement,* connected so strangely with the history of Provençal poetry, is deeply tinged with it. A touch of it makes the Franciscan order, with its poetry, its mysticism, its 'illumination,' from the point of view of religious authority, justly suspect. It influences the thoughts of those obscure prophetical writers, like Joachim of Flora,* strange dreamers in a world of flowery rhetoric of that third and final dispensation of a 'spirit of freedom,' in which law shall have passed away. Of this spirit *Aucassin and Nicolette* contains perhaps the most famous expression: it is the answer Aucassin gives when he is threatened with the pains of hell, if he makes Nicolette his mistress. A creature wholly of affection and the senses, he sees on the way to paradise only a feeble and worn-out company of aged priests, 'clinging day and night to the chapel altars,' barefoot or in patched sandals. With or even without Nicolette, 'his sweet mistress whom he so much loves,' he, for his part, is ready to start on the way to hell, along with 'the good scholars,' as he says, and the actors, and the fine horsemen dead in battle, and the men of fashion[1], and 'the fair courteous ladies who had two or three chevaliers apiece beside their own true lords,' all gay with music, in their gold, and silver, and beautiful furs—'the vair and the grey.'

But in the *House Beautiful** the saints too have their place; and the student of the Renaissance has this advantage over the student of the emancipation of the human mind in the Reformation, or the French Revolution, that in tracing the footsteps of humanity to higher levels, he is not beset at every turn by the inflexibilities and antagonisms of some well-recognised controversy, with rigidly defined opposites, exhausting the intelligence and limiting one's sympathies. The opposition of the professional defenders of a mere system to that more sincere and generous play of the forces of human mind and character, which I have noted as the secret of Abelard's struggle, is indeed always powerful. But the incompatibility with one another of souls really 'fair' is not essential; and within the enchanted region of the Renaissance, one needs not be for ever on one's guard. Here there are no fixed parties, no exclusions: all breathes of that unity of culture in which 'whatsoever things are comely' are reconciled, for the elevation and adorning of our spirits. And just in proportion as those who took part in the Renaissance become centrally representative of it, just so much the more is this condition realised in them. The wicked popes, and the loveless tyrants, who from time to time became its patrons, or mere speculators in its fortunes, lend themselves easily to disputations, and, from this side or that, the spirit of controversy lays just hold upon them. But the painter of the

---

[1] *Parage*, peerage:—which came to signify all that ambitious youth affected most on the outside of life, in that old world of the Troubadours, with whom this term is of frequent recurrence.

Last Supper,* with his kindred, lives in a land where controversy has no breathing-place. They refuse to be classified. In
the story of *Aucassin and Nicolette,* in the literature which it
represents, the note of defiance, of the opposition of one
system to another, is sometimes harsh. Let me conclude then
with a morsel from *Amis and Amile,* in which the harmony of
human interests is still entire. For the story of the great
traditional friendship, in which, as I said, the liberty of the
heart makes itself felt, seems, as we have it, to have been
written by a monk:—*La vie des saints martyrs Amis et Amile.** It
was not till the end of the seventeenth century that their
names were finally excluded from the martyrology; and their
story ends with this monkish miracle of earthly comradeship,
more than faithful unto death.—

'For, as God had united them in their lives in one accord,
so they were not divided in their death, falling together side
by side, with a host of other brave men, in battle for King
Charles at Mortara, so called from that great slaughter. And
the bishops gave counsel to the king and queen that they
should bury the dead, and build a church in that place; and
their counsel pleased the king greatly. And there were built
two churches, the one by commandment of the king in
honour of Saint Oseige, and the other by commandment of
the queen in honour of Saint Peter.

'And the king caused the two chests of stone to be brought
in the which the bodies of Amis and Amile lay; and Amile
was carried to the church of Saint Peter, and Amis to the
church of Saint Oseige; and the other corpses were buried,
some in one place and some in the other. But lo! next
morning, the body of Amile in his coffin was found lying in
the church of Saint Oseige, beside the coffin of Amis his
comrade. Behold then this wondrous amity, which by death
could not be dissevered!

'This miracle God did, who gave to His disciples power to
remove mountains. And by reason of this miracle the king
and queen remained in that place for a space of thirty days,
and performed the offices of the dead who were slain, and
honoured the said churches with great gifts. And the bishop

ordained many clerks to serve in the church of Saint Oseige, and commanded them that they should guard duly, with great devotion, the bodies of the two companions, Amis and Amile.'

1872.

PICO DELLA MIRANDOLA

No account of the Renaissance can be complete without some notice of the attempt made by certain Italian scholars of the fifteenth century to reconcile Christianity with the religion of ancient Greece. To reconcile forms of sentiment which at first sight seem incompatible, to adjust the various products of the human mind to one another in one many-sided type of intellectual culture, to give humanity, for heart and imagination to feed upon, as much as it could possibly receive, belonged to the generous instincts of that age. An earlier and simpler generation had seen in the gods of Greece so many malignant spirits, the defeated but still living centres of the religion of darkness, struggling, not always in vain, against the kingdom of light. Little by little, as the natural charm of pagan story reasserted itself over minds emerging out of barbarism, the religious significance which had once belonged to it was lost sight of, and it came to be regarded as the subject of a purely artistic or poetical treatment. But it was inevitable that from time to time minds should arise, deeply enough impressed by its beauty and power to ask themselves whether the religion of Greece was indeed a rival of the religion of Christ; for the older gods had rehabilitated themselves, and men's allegiance was divided. And the fifteenth century was an impassioned age, so ardent and serious in its pursuit of art that it consecrated everything with which art had to do as a religious object. The restored Greek literature had made it familiar, at least in Plato, with a style of expression concerning the earlier gods, which had about it something of the warmth and unction of a Christian hymn. It was too familiar with such language to regard mythology as a mere story; and it was too serious to play with a religion.

'Let me briefly remind the reader'—says Heine, in the *Gods in Exile*,* an essay full of that strange blending of sentiment which is characteristic of the traditions of the middle age concerning the pagan religions—'how the gods of the older world, at the time of the definite triumph of Christianity, that is, in the third century, fell into painful embarrassments, which greatly resembled certain tragical situations of their earlier life. They now found themselves beset by the same troublesome necessities to which they had once before been exposed during the primitive ages, in that revolutionary epoch when the Titans broke out of the custody of Orcus, and, piling Pelion on Ossa, scaled Olympus. Unfortunate gods! They had then to take flight ignominiously, and hide themselves among us here on earth, under all sorts of disguises. The larger number betook themselves to Egypt, where for greater security they assumed the forms of animals, as is generally known. Just in the same way, they had to take flight again, and seek entertainment in remote hiding-places, when those iconoclastic zealots, the black brood of monks, broke down all the temples, and pursued the gods with fire and curses. Many of these unfortunate emigrants, now entirely deprived of shelter and ambrosia, must needs take to vulgar handicrafts, as a means of earning their bread. Under these circumstances, many whose sacred groves had been confiscated, let themselves out for hire as woodcutters in Germany, and were forced to drink beer instead of nectar. Apollo seems to have been content to take service under graziers, and as he had once kept the cows of Admetus, so he lived now as a shepherd in Lower Austria. Here, however, having become suspected on account of his beautiful singing, he was recognised by a learned monk as one of the old pagan gods, and handed over to the spiritual tribunal. On the rack he confessed that he was the god Apollo; and before his execution he begged that he might be suffered to play once more upon the lyre, and to sing a song. And he played so touchingly, and sang with such magic, and was withal so beautiful in form and feature, that all the women wept, and many of them were so deeply impressed that they shortly afterwards fell sick. Some time afterwards the people wished to drag him from the grave again, that a stake might be driven through his body, in the belief that he had been a vampire, and that the sick women would by this means recover. But they found the grave empty.'

The Renaissance of the fifteenth century was, in many things, great rather by what it designed than by what it achieved. Much which it aspired to do, and did but imperfectly or mistakenly, was accomplished in what is called the *éclaircissement** of the eighteenth century, or in our own generation; and what really belongs to the revival of the fifteenth century is but the leading instinct, the curiosity, the initiatory idea. It is so with this very question of the reconciliation of the religion of antiquity with the religion of Christ. A modern scholar occupied by this problem might observe that all religions may be regarded as natural products, that, at least in their origin, their growth, and decay, they have common laws, and are not to be isolated from the other movements of the human mind in the periods in which they respectively prevailed; that they arise spontaneously out of the human mind, as expressions of the varying phases of its sentiment concerning the unseen world; that every intellectual product must be judged from the point of view of the age and the people in which it was produced. He might go on to observe that each has contributed something to the development of the religious sense, and ranging them as so many stages in the gradual education of the human mind, justify the existence of each. The basis of the reconciliation of the religions of the world would thus be the inexhaustible activity and creativeness of the human mind itself, in which all religions alike have their root, and in which all alike are reconciled; just as the fancies of childhood and the thoughts of old age meet and are laid to rest, in the experience of the individual.

Far different was the method followed by the scholars of the fifteenth century. They lacked the very rudiments of the historic sense, which, by an imaginative act, throws itself back into a world unlike one's own, and estimates every intellectual creation in its connexion with the age from which it proceeded. They had no idea of development, of the differences of ages, of the process by which our race has been 'educated.' In their attempts to reconcile the religions of the world, they were thus thrown back upon the quicksand of allegorical interpretation. The religions of the world were to be reconciled, not as successive stages in a regular development of the religious sense, but as subsisting side by side, and substantially in agreement with one another. And here the first necessity was to misrepresent the language, the conceptions, the sentiments, it was proposed to compare and reconcile. Plato and Homer must be made to speak agreeably to Moses. Set side by side, the mere surfaces could never unite in any harmony of design. Therefore one must go below the surface, and bring up the supposed secondary, or still more remote meaning,—that diviner signification held in reserve, *in recessu divinius aliquid*,* latent in some stray touch of Homer, or figure of speech in the books of Moses.

And yet as a curiosity of the human mind, a 'madhouse-cell,'* if you will, into which we may peep for a moment, and see it at work weaving strange fancies, the allegorical interpretation of the fifteenth century has its interest. With its strange web of imagery, its quaint conceits, its unexpected combinations and subtle moralising, it is an element in the local colour of a great age. It illustrates also the faith of that age in all oracles, its desire to hear all voices, its generous belief that nothing which had ever interested the human mind could wholly lose its vitality. It is the counterpart, though certainly the feebler counterpart, of that practical truce and reconciliation of the gods of Greece with the Christian religion, which is seen in the art of the time. And it is for his share in this work, and because his own story is a sort of analogue or visible equivalent to the expression of this purpose in his writings, that something of a general interest still belongs to the name of Pico della Mirandola, whose life, written by his nephew Francis, seemed worthy, for some touch of sweetness in it, to be translated out of the original Latin by Sir Thomas More, that great lover of Italian culture, among whose works the life of Pico, *Earl of Mirandola, and a great lord of Italy*, as he calls him, may still be read, in its quaint, antiquated English.

Marsilio Ficino* has told us how Pico came to Florence. It was the very day—some day probably in the year 1482—on which Ficino had finished his famous translation of Plato into Latin, the work to which he had been dedicated from

childhood by Cosmo de' Medici, in furtherance of his desire
to resuscitate the knowledge of Plato among his fellow-
citizens. Florence indeed, as M. Renan has pointed out,*
had always had an affinity for the mystic and dreamy
philosophy of Plato, while the colder and more practical
philosophy of Aristotle had flourished in Padua, and other
cities of the north; and the Florentines, though they knew
perhaps very little about him, had had the name of the great
idealist often on their lips. To increase this knowledge,
Cosmo had founded the Platonic academy, with periodical
discussions at the Villa Careggi. The fall of Constantinople
in 1453, and the council in 1438 for the reconcilation of the
Greek and Latin Churches, had brought to Florence many a
needy Greek scholar. And now the work was completed, the
door of the mystical temple lay open to all who could
construe Latin, and the scholar rested from his labour; when
there was introduced into his study, where a lamp burned
continually before the bust of Plato, as other men burned
lamps before their favourite saints, a young man fresh from
a journey, 'of feature and shape seemly and beauteous, of
stature goodly and high, of flesh tender and soft, his visage
lovely and fair, his colour white, intermingled with comely
reds, his eyes grey, and quick of look, his teeth white and
even, his hair yellow and abundant,' and trimmed with more
than the usual artifice of the time.

It is thus that Sir Thomas More translates the words of the
biographer of Pico, who, even in outward form and appearance, seems an image of that inward harmony and completeness, of which he is so perfect an example. The word *mystic*
has been usually derived from a Greek word which signifies
to shut, as if one *shut one's lips*, brooding on what cannot be
uttered; but the Platonists themselves derive it rather from
the act of *shutting the eyes*, that one may see the more,
inwardly. Perhaps the eyes of the mystic Ficino, now long
past the midway of life, had come to be thus half-closed; but
when a young man, not unlike the archangel Raphael, as the
Florentines of that age depicted him in his wonderful walk
with Tobit, or Mercury, as he might have appeared in a
painting by Sandro Botticelli or Piero di Cosimo, entered his

chamber, he seems to have thought there was something not wholly earthly about him; at least, he ever afterwards believed that it was not without the co-operation of the stars that the stranger had arrived on that day. For it happened that they fell into a conversation, deeper and more intimate than men usually fall into at first sight. During this conversation Ficino formed the design of devoting his remaining years to the translation of Plotinus, that new Plato, in whom the mystical element in the Platonic philosophy had been worked out to the utmost limit of vision and ecstasy; and it is in dedicating this translation to Lorenzo de' Medici that Ficino has recorded these incidents.

It was after many wanderings, wanderings of the intellect as well as physical journeys, that Pico came to rest at Florence. Born in 1463, he was then about twenty years old. He was called Giovanni at baptism, Pico, like all his ancestors, from Picus, nephew of the Emperor Constantine, from whom they claimed to be descended, and Mirandola from the place of his birth, a little town afterwards part of the duchy of Modena, of which small territory his family had long been the feudal lords. Pico was the youngest of the family, and his mother, delighting in his wonderful memory, sent him at the age of fourteen to the famous school of law at Bologna. From the first, indeed, she seems to have had some presentiment of his future fame, for, with a faith in omens characteristic of her time, she believed that a strange circumstance had happened at the time of Pico's birth—the appearance of a circular flame which suddenly vanished away, on the wall of the chamber where she lay. He remained two years at Bologna; and then, with an inexhaustible, unrivalled thirst for knowledge, the strange, confused, uncritical learning of that age, passed through the principal schools of Italy and France, penetrating, as he thought, into the secrets of all ancient philosophies, and many eastern languages. And with this flood of erudition came the generous hope, so often disabused, of reconciling the philosophers with one another, and all alike with the Church. At last he came to Rome. There, like some knight-errant of philosophy, he offered to defend nine hundred bold paradoxes, drawn from the most

opposite sources, against all comers. But the pontifical court
was led to suspect the orthodoxy of some of these proposi-
tions, and even the reading of the book which contained
them was forbidden by the Pope. It was not until 1493 that
Pico was finally absolved, by a brief of Alexander the Sixth.
Ten years before that date he had arrived at Florence; an
early instance of those who, after following the vain hope of
an impossible reconciliation from system to system, have at
last fallen back unsatisfied on the simplicities of their childhood's belief.

The oration which Pico composed for the opening of this
philosophical tournament still remains; its subject is the
dignity of human nature, the greatness of man. In common
with nearly all medieval speculation, much of Pico's writing
has this for its drift; and in common also with it, Pico's
theory of that dignity is founded on a misconception of the
place in nature both of the earth and of man. For Pico the
earth is the centre of the universe: and around it, as a fixed
and motionless point, the sun and moon and stars revolve,
like diligent servants or ministers. And in the midst of all is
placed man, *nodus et vinculum mundi*, the bond or copula of the
world, and the 'interpreter of nature': that famous expression of Bacon's really belongs to Pico. *Tritum est in scholis*, he
says, *esse hominem minorem mundum, in quo mixtum ex elementis
corpus et spiritus coelestis et plantarum anima vegetalis et brutorum
sensus et ratio et angelica mens et Dei similitudo conspicitur*:—'It is a
commonplace of the schools that man is a little world, in
which we may discern a body mingled of earthy elements,
and ethereal breath, and the vegetable life of plants, and the
senses of the lower animals, and reason, and the intelligence
of angels, and a likeness to God.'

A commonplace of the schools! But perhaps it had some
new significance and authority, when men heard one like
Pico reiterate it; and, false as its basis was, the theory had its
use. For this high dignity of man, thus bringing the dust
under his feet into sensible communion with the thoughts
and affections of the angels, was supposed to belong to him,
not as renewed by a religious system, but by his own natural
right. The proclamation of it was a counterpoise to the

increasing tendency of medieval religion to depreciate man's nature, to sacrifice this or that element in it, to make it ashamed of itself, to keep the degrading or painful accidents of it always in view. It helped man onward to that reassertion of himself, that rehabilitation of human nature, the body, the senses, the heart, the intelligence, which the Renaissance fulfils. And yet to read a page of one of Pico's forgotten books is like a glance into one of those ancient sepulchres, upon which the wanderer in classical lands has sometimes stumbled, with the old disused ornaments and furniture of a world wholly unlike ours still fresh in them. That whole conception of nature is so different from our own. For Pico the world is a limited place, bounded by actual crystal walls, and a material firmament; it is like a painted toy, like that map or system of the world, held, as a great target or shield, in the hands of the creative *Logos*, by whom the Father made all things, in one of the earlier frescoes of the *Campo Santo* at Pisa. How different from this childish dream is our own conception of nature, with its unlimited space, its innumerable suns, and the earth but a mote in the beam; how different the strange new awe, or superstition, with which it fills our minds! 'The silence of those infinite spaces,' says Pascal, contemplating a starlight night, 'the silence of those infinite spaces terrifies me:'—*Le silence éternel de ces espaces infinis m'effraie.*

He was already almost wearied out when he came to Florence. He had loved much and been beloved by women, 'wandering over the crooked hills of delicious pleasure;' but their reign over him was over, and long before Savonarola's famous 'bonfire of vanities,'* he had destroyed those love-songs in the vulgar tongue, which would have been so great a relief to us, after the scholastic prolixity of his Latin writings. It was in another spirit that he composed a Platonic commentary, the only work of his in Italian which has come down to us, on the 'Song of Divine Love'—*secondo la mente ed opinione dei Platonici*—'according to the mind and opinion of the Platonists,' by his friend Hieronymo Beniveni, in which, with an ambitious array of every sort of learning, and a profusion of imagery borrowed indifferently from the

astrologers, the Cabala, and Homer, and Scripture, and
Dionysius the Areopagite, he attempts to define the stages by
which the soul passes from the earthly to the unseen beauty.
A change indeed had passed over him, as if the chilling touch
of the abstract and disembodied beauty Platonists profess to
long for were already upon him. Some sense of this, perhaps,
coupled with that over-brightness which in the popular
imagination always betokens an early death, made Camilla
Rucellai, one of those prophetic women whom the preaching
of Savonarola had raised up in Florence, declare, seeing him
for the first time, that he would depart in the time of lilies—
prematurely, that is, like the field-flowers which are withered
by the scorching sun almost as soon as they are sprung up.
He now wrote down those thoughts on the religious life
which Sir Thomas More turned into English, and which
another English translator thought worthy to be added to
the books of the *Imitation*. 'It is not hard to know God,
provided one will not force oneself to define Him:'—has
been thought a great saying of Joubert's. 'Love God,' Pico
writes to Angelo Politian, 'we rather may, than either know
Him, or by speech utter Him. And yet had men liefer by
knowledge never find that which they seek, than by love
possess that thing, which also without love were in vain
found.'

Yet he who had this fine touch for spiritual things did
not—and in this is the enduring interest of his story—even
after his conversion, forget the old gods. He is one of the last
who seriously and sincerely entertained the claim on men's
faith of the pagan religions; he is anxious to ascertain the
true significance of the obscurest legend, the lightest tradition concerning them. With many thoughts and many
influences which led him in that direction, he did not become
a monk; only he became gentle and patient in disputation;
retaining 'somewhat of the old plenty, in dainty viand and
silver vessel,' he gave over the greater part of his property to
his friend, the mystical poet Beniveni, to be spent by him in
works of charity, chiefly in the sweet charity of providing
marriage-dowries for the peasant girls of Florence. His end
came in 1494, when, amid the prayers and sacraments of

Savonarola, he died of fever, on the very day on which Charles the Eighth entered Florence, the seventeenth of November, yet in the time of lilies—the lilies of the shield of France, as the people now said, remembering Camilla's prophecy. He was buried in the conventual church of Saint Mark, in the hood and white frock of the Dominican order.

It is because the life of Pico, thus lying down to rest in the Dominican habit, yet amid thoughts of the older gods, himself like one of those comely divinities, reconciled indeed to the new religion, but still with a tenderness for the earlier life, and desirous literally to 'bind the ages each to each by natural piety'—it is because this life is so perfect a parallel to the attempt made in his writings to reconcile Christianity with the ideas of paganism, that Pico, in spite of the scholastic character of those writings, is really interesting. Thus, in the *Heptaplus, or Discourse on the Seven Days of the Creation*, he endeavours to reconcile the accounts which pagan philosophy had given of the origin of the world with the account given in the books of Moses—the *Timæus* of Plato with the book of *Genesis*. The *Heptaplus* is dedicated to Lorenzo the Magnificent, whose interest, the preface tells us, in the secret wisdom of Moses is well known. If Moses seems in his writings simple and even popular, rather than either a philosopher or a theologian, that is because it was an institution with the ancient philosophers, either not to speak of divine things at all, or to speak of them dissemblingly: hence their doctrines were called mysteries. Taught by them, Pythagoras became so great a 'master of silence,' and wrote almost nothing, thus hiding the words of God in his heart, and speaking wisdom only among the perfect. In explaining the harmony between Plato and Moses, Pico lays hold on every sort of figure and analogy, on the double meanings of words, the symbols of the Jewish ritual, the secondary meanings of obscure stories in the later Greek mythologists. Everywhere there is an unbroken system of correspondences. Every object in the terrestrial world is an analogue, a symbol or counterpart, of some higher reality in the starry heavens, and this again of some law of the angelic life in the world beyond the stars. There is the element of fire in the material world: the sun is the fire of heaven; and in the super-celestial world there is the fire of the seraphic intelligence. 'But behold how they differ! The elementary fire burns, the heavenly fire vivifies, the super-celestial fire loves.' In this way, every natural object, every combination of natural forces, every accident in the lives of men, is filled with higher meanings. Omens, prophecies, supernatural coincidences, accompany Pico himself all through life. There are oracles in every tree and mountain-top, and a significance in every accidental combination of the events of life.

This constant tendency to symbolism and imagery gives Pico's work a figured style, by which it has some real resemblance to Plato's, and he differs from other mystical writers of his time by a genuine desire to know his authorities at first hand. He reads Plato in Greek, Moses in Hebrew, and by this his work really belongs to the higher culture. Above all, we have a constant sense in reading him, that his thoughts, however little their positive value may be, are connected with springs beneath them of deep and passionate emotion; and when he explains the grades or steps by which the soul passes from the love of a physical object to the love of unseen beauty, and unfolds the analogies between this process and other movements upward of human thought, there is a glow and vehemence in his words which remind one of the manner in which his own brief existence flamed itself away.

I said that the Renaissance of the fifteenth century was, in many things, great rather by what it designed or aspired to do, than by what it actually achieved. It remained for a later age to conceive the true method of effecting a scientific reconciliation of Christian sentiment with the imagery, the legends, the theories about the world, of pagan poetry and philosophy. For that age the only possible reconciliation was an imaginative one, and resulted from the efforts of artists, trained in Christian schools, to handle pagan subjects; and of this artistic reconciliation work like Pico's was but the feebler counterpart. Whatever philosophers had to say on one side or the other, whether they were successful or not in their attempts to reconcile the old to the new, and to justify the expenditure of so much care and thought on the dreams of a dead faith, the imagery of the Greek religion, the direct charm of its story, were by artists valued and cultivated for their own sake. Hence a new sort of mythology, with a tone and qualities of its own. When the ship-load of sacred earth from the soil of Jerusalem was mingled with the common clay in the *Campo Santo* at Pisa, a new flower grew up from it, unlike any flower men had seen before, the anemone with its concentric rings of strangely blended colour, still to be found by those who search long enough for it, in the long grass of the Maremma. Just such a strange flower was that mythology of the Italian Renaissance, which grew up from the mixture of two traditions, two sentiments, the sacred and the profane. Classical story was regarded as so much imaginative material to be received and assimilated. It did not come into men's minds to ask curiously of science, concerning the origin of such story, its primary form and import, its meaning for those who projected it. The thing sank into their minds, to issue forth again with all the tangle about it of medieval sentiment and ideas. In the *Doni* Madonna in the *Tribune* of the *Uffizii*, Michelangelo actually brings the pagan religion, and with it the unveiled human form, the sleepy-looking fauns of a Dionysiac revel, into the presence of the Madonna, as simpler painters had introduced there other products of the earth, birds or flowers, while he has given to that Madonna herself much of the uncouth energy of the older and more primitive 'Mighty Mother.'

This picturesque union of contrasts, belonging properly to the art of the close of the fifteenth century, pervades, in Pico della Mirandola, an actual person, and that is why the figure of Pico is so attractive. He will not let one go; he wins one on, in spite of one's self, to turn again to the pages of his forgotten books, although we know already that the actual solution proposed in them will satisfy us as little as perhaps it satisfied him. It is said that in his eagerness for mysterious learning he once paid a great sum for a collection of cabalistic manuscripts, which turned out to be forgeries; and the story might well stand as a parable of all he ever seemed to gain in the way of actual knowledge. He had sought knowledge, and passed from system to system, and hazarded much; but less for the sake of positive knowledge than because he believed there was a spirit of order and beauty in knowledge, which would come down and unite what men's ignorance had divided, and renew what time had made dim. And so, while his actual work has passed away, yet his own qualities are still active, and himself remains, as one alive in the grave, *caesiis et vigilibus oculis*,* as his biographer describes him, and with that sanguine, clear skin, *decenti rubore interspersa*,* as with the light of morning upon it; and he has a true place in that group of great Italians who fill the end of the fifteenth century with their names, he is a true *humanist*. For the essence of humanism is that belief of which he seems never to have doubted, that nothing which has ever interested living men and women can wholly lose its vitality—no language they have spoken, nor oracle beside which they have hushed their voices, no dream which has once been entertained by actual human minds, nothing about which they have ever been passionate, or expended time and zeal.

1871.

SANDRO BOTTICELLI

In Leonardo's treatise on painting only one contemporary is mentioned by name—Sandro Botticelli. This pre-eminence may be due to chance only, but to some will rather appear a result of deliberate judgment; for people have begun to find out the charm of Botticelli's work, and his name, little known in the last century, is quietly becoming important. In the middle of the fifteenth century he had already anticipated much of that meditative subtlety, which is sometimes supposed peculiar to the great imaginative workmen of its close. Leaving the simple religion which had occupied the followers of Giotto for a century, and the simple naturalism which had grown out of it, a thing of birds and flowers only, he sought inspiration in what to him were works of the modern world, the writings of Dante and Boccaccio, and in new readings of his own of classical stories: or, if he painted religious incidents, painted them with an under-current of original sentiment, which touches you as the real matter of the picture through the veil of its ostensible subject. What is the peculiar sensation, what is the peculiar quality of pleasure, which his work has the property of exciting in us, and which we cannot get elsewhere? For this, especially when he has to speak of a comparatively unknown artist, is always the chief question which a critic has to answer.

In an age when the lives of artists were full of adventure, his life is almost colourless. Criticism indeed has cleared away much of the gossip which Vasari accumulated,* has touched the legend of Lippo and Lucrezia, and rehabilitated the character of Andrea del Castagno. But in Botticelli's case there is no legend to dissipate. He did not even go by his true name: Sandro is a nickname, and his true name is Filipepi, Botticelli being only the name of the goldsmith who first taught him art. Only two things happened to him, two things which he shared with other artists:—he was invited to Rome to paint in the Sistine Chapel, and he fell in later life under the influence of Savonarola, passing apparently almost out of men's sight in a sort of religious melancholy, which lasted till his death in 1515, according to the received date. Vasari says that he plunged into the study of Dante, and even wrote a comment on the *Divine Comedy*. But it seems strange that he should have lived on inactive so long; and one almost wishes that some document might come to light, which, fixing the date of his death earlier, might relieve one, in thinking of him, of his dejected old age.

He is before all things a poetical painter, blending the charm of story and sentiment, the medium of the art of poetry, with the charm of line and colour, the medium of abstract painting. So he becomes the illustrator of Dante. In a few rare examples of the edition of 1481, the blank spaces, left at the beginning of every canto for the hand of the illuminator, have been filled, as far as the nineteenth canto of the *Inferno*, with impressions of engraved plates, seemingly by way of experiment, for in the copy in the Bodleian Library, one of the three impressions it contains has been printed upside down, and much awry, in the midst of the luxurious printed page. Giotto, and the followers of Giotto, with their almost childish religious aim, had not learned to put that weight of meaning into outward things, light, colour, everyday gesture, which the poetry of the *Divine Comedy* involves, and before the fifteenth century Dante could hardly have found an illustrator. Botticelli's illustrations are crowded with incident, blending, with a naïve carelessness of pictorial propriety, three phases of the same scene into one plate. The grotesques, so often a stumbling-block to painters, who forget that the words of a poet, which only feebly present an image to the mind, must be lowered in key when translated into visible form, make one regret that he has not rather chosen for illustration the more subdued imagery of the *Purgatorio*. Yet in the scene of those who 'go down quick into hell,' there is an inventive force about the fire taking hold on the upturned soles of the feet, which proves that the design is no mere translation of Dante's words, but a true painter's vision; while the scene of the Centaurs wins one at once, for, forgetful of the actual circumstances of their appearance, Botticelli has gone off with delight on the thought of the Centaurs themselves, bright, small creatures of the woodland, with arch baby faces and mignon forms, drawing tiny bows.

Botticelli lived in a generation of naturalists, and he might have been a mere naturalist among them. There are traces enough in his work of that alert sense of outward things, which, in the pictures of that period, fills the lawns with delicate living creatures, and the hillsides with pools of water, and the pools of water with flowering reeds. But this was not enough for him; he is a visionary painter, and in his visionariness he resembles Dante. Giotto, the tried companion of Dante, Masaccio, Ghirlandajo even, do but transcribe, with more or less refining, the outward image; they are dramatic, not visionary painters; they are almost impassive spectators of the action before them. But the genius of which Botticelli is the type usurps the data before it as the exponent of ideas, moods, visions of its own; in this interest it plays fast and loose with those data, rejecting some and isolating others, and always combining them anew. To him, as to Dante, the scene, the colour, the outward image or gesture, comes with all its incisive and importunate reality; but awakes in him, moreover, by some subtle law of his own structure, a mood which it awakes in no one else, of which it is the double or repetition, and which it clothes, that all may share it, with visible circumstance.

But he is far enough from accepting the conventional orthodoxy of Dante which, referring all human action to the simple formula of purgatory, heaven and hell, leaves an insoluble element of prose in the depths of Dante's poetry. One picture of his, with the portrait of the donor, Matteo Palmieri, below, had the credit or discredit of attracting some shadow of ecclesiastical censure. This Matteo Palmieri, (two dim figures move under that name in contemporary history,) was the reputed author of a poem, still unedited, *La Città Divina*, which represented the human race as an incarnation of those angels who, in the revolt of Lucifer, were neither for Jehovah nor for His enemies, a fantasy of that earlier Alexandrian philosophy about which the Florentine intellect in that century was so curious. Botticelli's picture may have been only one of those familiar compositions in which religious reverie has recorded its impressions of the various forms of beatified existence—*Glorias*, as they were called, like that in which Giotto painted the portrait of Dante; but somehow it was suspected of embodying in a picture the wayward dream of Palmieri, and the chapel where it hung was closed. Artists so entire as Botticelli are usually careless about philosophical theories, even when the philosopher is a Florentine of the fifteenth century, and his work a poem in *terza rima*. But Botticelli, who wrote a commentary on Dante, and became the disciple of Savonarola, may well have let such theories come and go across him. True or false, the story interprets much of the peculiar sentiment with which he infuses his profane and sacred persons, comely, and in a certain sense like angels, but with a sense of displacement or loss about them—the wistfulness of exiles, conscious of a passion and energy greater than any known issue of them explains, which runs through all his varied work with a sentiment of ineffable melancholy.

So just what Dante scorns as unworthy alike of heaven and hell, Botticelli accepts, that middle world in which men take no side in great conflicts, and decide no great causes, and make great refusals. He thus sets for himself the limits within which art, undisturbed by any moral ambition, does its most sincere and surest work. His interest is neither in the untempered goodness of Angelico's saints, nor the untempered evil of Orcagna's *Inferno*; but with men and women, in their mixed and uncertain condition, always attractive, clothed sometimes by passion with a character of loveliness and energy, but saddened perpetually by the shadow upon them of the great things from which they shrink. His morality is all sympathy; and it is this sympathy, conveying into his work somewhat more than is usual of the true complexion of humanity, which makes him, visionary as he is, so forcible a realist.

It is this which gives to his Madonnas their unique expression and charm. He has worked out in them a distinct and peculiar type, definite enough in his own mind, for he has painted it over and over again, sometimes one might think almost mechanically, as a pastime during that dark period when his thoughts were so heavy upon him. Hardly any collection of note is without one of these circular pictures, into which the attendant angels depress their heads so naïvely. Perhaps you have sometimes wondered why those peevish-looking Madonnas, conformed to no acknowledged or obvious type of beauty, attract you more and more, and often come back to you when the Sistine Madonna and the Virgins of Fra Angelico are forgotten. At first, contrasting them with those, you may have thought that there was something in them mean or abject even, for the abstract lines of the face have little nobleness, and the colour is wan. For with Botticelli she too, though she holds in her hands the 'Desire of all nations,'* is one of those who are neither for Jehovah nor for His enemies; and her choice is on her face. The white light on it is cast up hard and cheerless from below, as when snow lies upon the ground, and the children look up with surprise at the strange whiteness of the ceiling. Her trouble is in the very caress of the mysterious child, whose gaze is always far from her, and who has already that sweet look of devotion which men have never been able altogether to love, and which still makes the born saint an object almost of suspicion to his earthly brethren. Once, indeed, he guides her hand to transcribe in a book the words of her exaltation, the *Ave*, and the *Magnificat*, and the *Gaude Maria*, and the young angels, glad to rouse her for a moment from her dejection, are eager to hold the inkhorn and to support the book. But the pen almost drops from her hand, and the high cold words have no meaning for her, and her true children are those others, among whom, in her rude home, the intolerable honour came to her, with that look of wistful inquiry on their irregular faces which you see in startled animals—gipsy children, such as those who, in Apennine villages, still hold out their long brown arms to beg of you, but on Sundays become *enfants du chœur*,* with their thick black hair nicely combed, and fair white linen on their sunburnt throats.

What is strangest is that he carries this sentiment into classical subjects, its most complete expression being a

picture in the *Uffizii*, of Venus rising from the sea, in which
the grotesque emblems of the middle age, and a landscape
full of its peculiar feeling, and even its strange draperies,
powdered all over in the Gothic manner with a quaint
conceit of daisies, frame a figure that reminds you of the
faultless nude studies of Ingres. At first, perhaps, you are
attracted only by a quaintness of design, which seems to
recall all at once whatever you have read of Florence in the
fifteenth century; afterwards you may think that this quaintness must be incongruous with the subject, and that the
colour is cadaverous or at least cold. And yet, the more you
come to understand what imaginative colouring really is,
that all colour is no mere delightful quality of natural things,
but a spirit upon them by which they become expressive to
the spirit, the better you will like this peculiar quality of
colour; and you will find that quaint design of Botticelli's a
more direct inlet into the Greek temper than the works of the
Greeks themselves even of the finest period. Of the Greeks as
they really were, of their difference from ourselves, of the
aspects of their outward life, we know far more than
Botticelli, or his most learned contemporaries; but for us long
familiarity has taken off the edge of the lesson, and we are
hardly conscious of what we owe to the Hellenic spirit. But in
pictures like this of Botticelli's you have a record of the first
impression made by it on minds turned back towards it, in
almost painful aspiration, from a world in which it had been
ignored so long; and in the passion, the energy, the industry
of realisation, with which Botticelli carries out his intention,
is the exact measure of the legitimate influence over the
human mind of the imaginative system of which this is
perhaps the central subject. The light is indeed cold—mere
sunless dawn; but a later painter would have cloyed you with
sunshine; and you can see the better for that quietness in the
morning air each long promontory, as it slopes down to the
water's edge. Men go forth to their labours until the evening;
but she is awake before them, and you might think that the
sorrow in her face was at the thought of the whole long day
of love yet to come. An emblematical figure of the wind
blows hard across the grey water, moving forward the

dainty-lipped shell on which she sails, the sea 'showing his teeth,' as it moves, in thin lines of foam, and sucking in, one by one, the falling roses, each severe in outline, plucked off short at the stalk, but embrowned a little, as Botticelli's flowers always are. Botticelli meant all this imagery to be altogether pleasurable; and it was partly an incompleteness of resources, inseparable from the art of that time, that subdued and chilled it. But his predilection for minor tones counts also; and what is unmistakable is the sadness with which he has conceived the goddess of pleasure, as the depository of a great power over the lives of men.

I have said that the peculiar character of Botticelli is the result of a blending in him of a sympathy for humanity in its uncertain condition, its attractiveness, its investiture at rarer moments in a character of loveliness and energy, with his consciousness of the shadow upon it of the great things from which it shrinks, and that this conveys into his work some-what more than painting usually attains of the true com-plexion of humanity. He paints the story of the goddess of pleasure in other episodes besides that of her birth from the sea, but never without some shadow of death in the grey flesh and wan flowers. He paints Madonnas, but they shrink from the pressure of the divine child, and plead in unmistak-able undertones for a warmer, lower humanity. The same figure—tradition connects it with Simonetta,* the mistress of Giuliano de' Medici—appears again as Judith, returning home across the hill country, when the great deed is over, and the moment of revulsion come, when the olive branch in her hand is becoming a burthen; as *Justice*, sitting on a throne, but with a fixed look of self-hatred which makes the sword in her hand seem that of a suicide; and again as *Veritas*, in the allegorical picture of *Calumnia*,* where one may note in passing the suggestiveness of an accident which identifies the image of Truth with the person of Venus. We might trace the same sentiment through his engravings; but his share in them is doubtful, and the object of this brief study has been attained, if I have defined aright the temper in which he worked.

But, after all, it may be asked, is a painter like

Botticelli—a secondary painter, a proper subject for general criticism? There are a few great painters, like Michelangelo or Leonardo, whose work has become a force in general culture, partly for this very reason that they have absorbed into themselves all such workmen as Sandro Botticelli; and, over and above mere technical or antiquarian criticism, general criticism may be very well employed in that sort of interpretation which adjusts the position of these men to general culture, whereas smaller men can be the proper subjects only of technical or antiquarian treatment. But, besides those great men, there is a certain number of artists who have a distinct faculty of their own by which they convey to us a peculiar quality of pleasure which we cannot get elsewhere; and these too have their place in general culture, and must be interpreted to it by those who have felt their charm strongly, and are often the object of a special diligence and a consideration wholly affectionate, just because there is not about them the stress of a great name and authority. Of this select number Botticelli is one. He has the freshness, the uncertain and diffident promise, which belong to the earlier Renaissance period itself, and make it perhaps the most interesting period in the history of the mind. In studying his work one begins to understand to how great a place in human culture the art of Italy had been called.

1870.

LUCA DELLA ROBBIA

The Italian sculptors of the earlier half of the fifteenth century are more than mere forerunners of the great masters of its close, and often reach perfection, within the narrow limits which they chose to impose on their work. Their sculpture shares with the paintings of Botticelli and the churches of Brunelleschi that profound expressiveness, that intimate impress of an indwelling soul, which is the peculiar fascination of the art of Italy in that century. Their works have been much neglected, and often almost hidden away amid the frippery of modern decoration, and we come with some surprise on the places where their fire still smoulders. One longs to penetrate into the lives of the men who have given expression to so much power and sweetness. But it is part of the reserve, the austere dignity and simplicity of their existence, that their histories are for the most part lost, or told but briefly. From their lives, as from their work, all tumult of sound and colour has passed away. Mino, the Raphael of sculpture, Maso del Rodario, whose works add a further grace to the church of Como, Donatello even,—one asks in vain for more than a shadowy outline of their actual days.

Something more remains of Luca della Robbia; something more of a history, of outward changes and fortunes, is expressed through his work. I suppose nothing brings the real air of a Tuscan town so vividly to mind as those pieces of pale blue and white earthenware, by which he is best known, like fragments of the milky sky itself, fallen into the cool streets, and breaking into the darkened churches. And no work is less imitable: like Tuscan wine, it loses its savour when moved from its birthplace, from the crumbling walls where it was first placed. Part of the charm of this work, its grace and purity and finish of expression, is common to all the Tuscan sculptors of the fifteenth century; for Luca was first of all a worker in marble, and his works in *terra cotta* only transfer to a different material the principles of his sculpture.

These Tuscan sculptors of the fifteenth century worked for the most part in low relief, giving even to their monumental effigies something of its depression of surface, getting into them by this means a pathetic suggestion of the wasting and etherealisation of death. They are haters of all heaviness and emphasis, of strongly-opposed light and shade, and seek their means of delineation among those last refinements of shadow, which are almost invisible except in a strong light, and which the finest pencil can hardly follow. The whole essence of their work is *expression*, the passing of a smile over the face of a child, the ripple of the air on a still day over the curtain of a window ajar.

What is the precise value of this system of sculpture, this low relief? Luca della Robbia, and the other sculptors of the school to which he belongs, have before them the universal problem of their art; and this system of low relief is the means by which they meet and overcome the special limitation of sculpture.

That limitation results from the material, and other necessary conditions, of all sculptured work, and consists in the tendency of such work to a hard realism, a one-sided presentment of mere form, that solid material frame which only motion can relieve, a thing of heavy shadows, and an individuality of expression pushed to caricature. Against this tendency to the hard presentment of mere form trying vainly to compete with the reality of nature itself, all noble sculpture constantly struggles; each great system of sculpture resisting, it in its own way, etherealising, spiritualising, relieving, its stiffness, its heaviness, and death. The use of colour in sculpture is but an unskilful contrivance to effect, by borrowing from another art, what the nobler sculpture effects by strictly appropriate means. To get not colour, but the equivalent of colour; to secure the expression and the play of life; to expand the too firmly fixed individuality of pure, unrelieved, uncoloured form:—this is the problem which the three great styles in sculpture have solved in three different ways.

Allgemeinheit—breadth, generality, universality—is the word chosen by Winckelmann, and after him by Goethe and

many German critics, to express that law of the most
excellent Greek sculptors, of Pheidias* and his pupils, which
prompted them constantly to seek the type in the individual,
to abstract and express only what is structural and permanent, to purge from the individual all that belongs only to
him, all the accidents, the feelings and actions of the special
moment, all that (because in its own nature it endures but
for a moment) is apt to look like a frozen thing if one arrests
it.

In this way their works came to be like some subtle extract
or essence, or almost like pure thoughts or ideas: and hence
the breadth of humanity in them, that detachment from the
conditions of a particular place or people, which has carried
their influence far beyond the age which produced them,
and insured them universal acceptance.

That was the Greek way of relieving the hardness and
unspirituality of pure form. But it involved to a certain
degree the sacrifice of what we call *expression*; and a system of
abstraction which aimed always at the broad and general
type, at the purging away from the individual of what
belonged only to him, and of the mere accidents of a
particular time and place, imposed upon the range of effects
open to the Greek sculptor limits somewhat narrowly
defined. When Michelangelo came, therefore, with a genius
spiritualised by the reverie of the middle age, penetrated by
its spirit of inwardness and introspection, living not a mere
outward life like the Greek, but a life full of intimate
experiences, sorrows, consolations, a system which sacrificed
so much of what was inward and unseen could not satisfy
him. To him, lover and student of Greek sculpture as he was,
work which did not bring what was inward to the surface,
which was not concerned with individual expression, with
individual character and feeling, the special history of the
special soul, was not worth doing at all.

And so, in a way quite personal and peculiar to himself,
which often is, and always seems, the effect of accident, he
secured for his work individuality and intensity of expression, while he avoided a too heavy realism, that tendency to
harden into caricature which the representation of feeling in

sculpture is apt to display. What time and accident, its centuries of darkness under the furrows of the 'little Melian farm,' have done with singular felicity of touch for the Venus of Melos,* fraying its surface and softening its lines, so that some spirit in the thing seems always on the point of breaking out, as though in it classical sculpture had advanced already one step into the mystical Christian age, its expression being in the whole range of ancient work most like that of Michelangelo's own:—this effect Michelangelo gains by leaving nearly all his sculpture in a puzzling sort of incompleteness, which suggests rather than realises actual form. Something of the wasting of that snow-image* which he moulded at the command of Piero de' Medici, when the snow lay one night in the court of the *Pitti* palace, almost always lurks about it, as if he had determined to make the quality of a task, exacted from him half in derision, the pride of all his work. Many have wondered at that incompleteness, suspecting, however, that Michelangelo himself loved and was loath to change it, and feeling at the same time that they too would lose something if the half-realised form ever quite emerged from the stone, so rough-hewn here, so delicately finished there; and they have wished to fathom the charm of this incompleteness. Well! that incompleteness is Michelangelo's equivalent for colour in sculpture; it is his way of etherealising pure form, of relieving its stiff realism, and communicating to it breath, pulsation, the effect of life. It was a characteristic too which fell in with his peculiar temper and mode of living, his disappointments and hesitations. And it was in reality perfect finish. In this way he combines the utmost amount of passion and intensity with the sense of a yielding and flexible life: he gets not vitality merely, but a wonderful force, of expression.

Midway between these two systems—the system of the Greek sculptors and the system of Michelangelo—comes the system of Luca della Robbia and the other Tuscan sculptors of the fifteenth century, partaking both of the *Allgemeinheit* of the Greeks, their way of extracting certain select elements only of pure form and sacrificing all the rest, and the studied incompleteness of Michelangelo, relieving that sense of intensity, passion, energy, which might otherwise have stiffened into caricature. Like Michelangelo, these sculptors fill their works with intense and individualised expression. Their noblest works are the careful sephulchral portraits of particular persons—the monument of Conte Ugo in the *Badía* of Florence, of the youthful Medea Colleoni, with the wonderful, long throat, in the chapel on the cool north side of the Church of *Santa Maria Maggiore* at Bergamo—monuments such as abound in the churches of Rome, inexhaustible in suggestions of repose, of a subdued sabbatic joy, a kind of sacred grace and refinement. And these elements of tranquillity, of repose, they unite to an intense and individual expression by a system of conventionalism as skilful and subtle as that of the Greeks, repressing all such curves as indicate solid form, and throwing the whole into low relief.

The life of Luca, a life of labour and frugality, with no adventure and no excitement except what belongs to the trial of new artistic processes, the struggle with new artistic difficulties, the solution of purely artistic problems, fills the first seventy years of the fifteenth century. After producing many works in marble for the *Duomo* and the *Campanile* of Florence, which place him among the foremost masters of the sculpture of his age, he became desirous to realise the spirit and manner of that sculpture, in a humbler material, to unite its science, its exquisite and expressive system of low relief, to the homely art of pottery, to introduce those high qualities into common things, to adorn and cultivate daily household life. In this he is profoundly characteristic of the Florence of that century, of that in it which lay below its superficial vanity and caprice, a certain old-world modesty and seriousness and simplicity. People had not yet begun to think that what was good art for churches was not so good, or less fitted, for their own houses. Luca's new work was in plain white earthenware at first, a mere rough imitation of the costly, laboriously wrought marble, finished in a few hours. But on this humble path he found his way to a fresh success, to another artistic grace. The fame of the oriental pottery, with its strange, bright colours—colours of art, colours not to be attained in the natural stone—mingled with the tradition of the old Roman pottery of the neigh-bourhood. The little red, coral-like jars of Arezzo, dug up in that district from time to time, are much prized. These colours haunted Luca's fancy. 'He still continued seeking something more,' his biographer says of him; 'and instead of making his figures of baked earth simply white, he added the further invention of giving them colour, to the astonishment and delight of all who beheld them'—*Cosa singolare, e multo utile per la state!*—a curious thing, and very useful for summer-time, full of coolness and repose for hand and eye. Luca loved the forms of various fruits, and wrought them into all sorts of marvellous frames and garlands, giving them their natural colours, only subdued a little, a little paler than nature.

I said that the art of Luca della Robbia possessed in an unusual measure that special characteristic which belongs to all the workmen of his school, a characteristic which, even in the absence of much positive information about their actual history, seems to bring those workmen themselves very near to us. They bear the impress of a personal quality, a profound expressiveness, what the French call *intimité*, by which is meant some subtler sense of originality—the seal on a man's work of what is most inward and peculiar in his moods, and manner of apprehension: it is what we call *expression*, carried to its highest intensity of degree. That characteristic is rare in poetry, rarer still in art, rarest of all in the abstract art of sculpture; yet essentially, perhaps, it is the quality which alone makes work in the imaginative order really worth having at all. It is because the works of the artists of the fifteenth century possess this quality in an unmistakable way that one is anxious to know all that can be known about them, and explain to one's self the secret of their charm.

1872.

THE POETRY OF MICHELANGELO

CRITICS of Michelangelo have sometimes spoken as if the only characteristic of his genius were a wonderful strength, verging, as in the things of the imagination great strength always does, on what is singular or strange. A certain strangeness, something of the blossoming of the aloe, is indeed an element in all true works of art: that they shall excite or surprise us is indispensable. But that they shall give pleasure and exert a charm over us is indispensable too; and this strangeness must be sweet also—a lovely strangeness. And to the true admirers of Michelangelo this is the true type of the Michelangelesque—sweetness and strength, pleasure with surprise, an energy of conception which seems at every moment about to break through all the conditions of comely form, recovering, touch by touch, a loveliness found usually only in the simplest natural things—*ex forti dulcedo*.*

In this way he sums up for them the whole character of medieval art itself in that which distinguishes it most clearly from classical work, the presence of a convulsive energy in it, becoming in lower hands merely monstrous or forbidding, and felt, even in its most graceful products, as a subdued quaintness or grotesque. Yet those who feel this grace or sweetness in Michelangelo might at the first moment be puzzled if they were asked wherein precisely such quality resided. Men of inventive temperament—Victor Hugo, for instance, in whom, as in Michelangelo, people have for the most part been attracted or repelled by the strength, while few have understood his sweetness—have sometimes relieved conceptions of merely moral or spiritual greatness, but with little æsthetic charm of their own, by lovely accidents or accessories, like the butterfly which alights on the blood-stained barricade in *Les Misérables*, or those sea-birds for whom the monstrous Gilliatt comes to be as some wild natural thing, so that they are no longer afraid of him, in *Les Travailleurs de la Mer*. But the austere genius of Michelangelo will not depend for its sweetness on any mere accessories like these. The world of natural things has almost no existence for him; 'When one speaks of him,' says Grimm,* 'woods, clouds, seas, and mountains disappear, and only what is formed by the spirit of man remains behind;' and he quotes a few slight words from a letter of his to Vasari as the single expression in all he has left of a feeling for nature. He has traced no flowers, like those with which Leonardo stars over his gloomiest rocks; nothing like the fretwork of wings and flames in which Blake frames his most startling conceptions. No forest-scenery like Titian's fills his backgrounds, but only blank ranges of rock, and dim vegetable forms as blank as they, as in a world before the creation of the first five days.

Of the whole story of the creation he has painted only the creation of the first man and woman, and, for him at least, feebly, the creation of light. It belongs to the quality of his genius thus to concern itself almost exclusively with the making of man. For him it is not, as in the story itself, the last and crowning act of a series of developments, but the first and unique act, the creation of life itself in its supreme form, off-hand and immediately, in the cold and lifeless stone. With him the beginning of life has all the characteristics of resurrection; it is like the recovery of suspended health or animation, with its gratitude, its effusion, and eloquence. Fair as the young men of the Elgin marbles, the Adam of the Sistine Chapel is unlike them in a total absence of that balance and completeness which express so well the sentiment of a self-contained, independent life. In that languid figure there is something rude and satyr-like, something akin to the rugged hillside on which it lies. His whole form is gathered into an expression of mere expectancy and reception; he has hardly strength enough to lift his finger to touch the finger of the creator; yet a touch of the finger-tips will suffice.

This creation of life—life coming always as relief or recovery, and always in strong contrast with the rough-hewn mass in which it is kindled—is in various ways the motive of all his work, whether its immediate subject be pagan or Christian, legend or allegory; and this, although at least one-half of his work was designed for the adornment of tombs—the tomb of Julius, the tombs of the Medici. Not the Judgment but the Resurrection is the real subject of his last work in the Sistine Chapel; and his favourite pagan subject is the legend of Leda, the delight of the world breaking from the egg of a bird. As I have already pointed out, he secures that ideality of expression which in Greek sculpture depends on a delicate system of abstraction, and in early Italian sculpture on lowness of relief, by an incompleteness, which is surely not always undesigned, and which, as I think, no one regrets, and trusts to the spectator to complete the half-emergent form. And as his persons have something of the unwrought stone about them, so, as if to realise the expression by which the old Florentine records describe a sculptor—*master of live stone*—with him the very rocks seem to have life. They have but to cast away the dust and scurf that they may rise and stand on their feet. He loved the very quarries of Carrara, those strange grey peaks which even at mid-day convey into any scene from which they are visible something of the solemnity and stillness of evening, sometimes wandering among them month after month, till at last their pale ashen colours seem to have passed into his painting; and on the crown of the head of the *David* there still remains a morsel of uncut stone, as if by one touch to maintain its connexion with the place from which it was hewn.

And it is in this penetrative suggestion of life that the secret of that sweetness of his is to be found. He gives us indeed no lovely natural objects like Leonardo or Titian, but only the coldest, most elementary shadowing of rock or tree; no lovely draperies and comely gestures of life, but only the austere truths of human nature; 'simple persons'—as he replied in his rough way to the querulous criticism of Julius the Second, that there was no gold on the figures of the Sistine Chapel—'simple persons, who wore no gold on their garments;' but he penetrates us with a feeling of that power which we associate with all the warmth and fulness of the world, the sense of which brings into one's thoughts a swarm of birds and flowers and insects. The brooding spirit of life itself is there; and the summer may burst out in a moment.

He was born in an interval of a rapid midnight journey in March, at a place in the neighbourhood of Arezzo, the thin, clear air of which was then thought to be favourable to the birth of children of great parts. He came of a race of grave and dignified men, who, claiming kinship with the family of Canossa, and some colour of imperial blood in their veins, had, generation after generation, received honourable employment under the government of Florence. His mother, a girl of nineteen years, put him out to nurse at a country-house among the hills of Settignano, where every other inhabitant is a worker in the marble-quarries, and the child early became familiar with that strange first stage in the sculptor's art. To this succeeded the influence of the sweetest and most placid master Florence had yet seen, Domenico Ghirlandajo. At fifteen he was at work among the curiosities of the garden of the Medici, copying and restoring antiques, winning the condescending notice of the great Lorenzo. He knew too how to excite strong hatreds; and it was at this time that in a quarrel with a fellow-student he received a blow on the face which deprived him for ever of the comeliness of outward form.

It was through an accident that he came to study those works of the early Italian sculptors which suggested much of his own grandest work, and impressed it with so deep a sweetness. He believed in dreams and omens. One of his friends dreamed twice that Lorenzo, then lately dead, appeared to him in grey and dusty apparel. To Michelangelo this dream seemed to portend the troubles which afterwards really came, and with the suddenness which was characteristic of all his movements, he left Florence. Having occasion to pass through Bologna, he neglected to procure the little seal of red wax which the stranger entering Bologna must carry on the thumb of his right hand. He had no money to pay the fine, and would have been thrown into prison had not one of the magistrates interposed. He remained in this man's house a whole year, rewarding his hospitality by readings from the Italian poets whom he loved. Bologna, with its endless colonnades and fantastic leaning towers, can never have been one of the lovelier cities of Italy. But about the portals of its vast unfinished churches and its dark shrines, half hidden by votive flowers and candles, lie some of the sweetest works of the early Tuscan sculptors, Giovanni da Pisa and Jacopo della Quercia, things as winsome as flowers; and the year which Michelangelo spent in copying these works was not a lost year. It was now, on returning to Florence, that he put forth that unique presentment of Bacchus,* which expresses, not the mirthfulness of the god of wine, but his sleepy seriousness, his enthusiasm, his capacity for profound dreaming. No one ever expressed more truly than Michelangelo the notion of inspired sleep, of faces charged with dreams. A vast fragment of marble had long lain below the *Loggia* of Orcagna, and many a sculptor had had his thoughts of a design which should just fill this famous block of stone, cutting the diamond, as it were, without loss. Under Michelangelo's hand it became the *David* which stood till lately on the steps of the *Palazzo Vecchio*, when it was replaced below the *Loggia*. Michelangelo was now thirty years old, and his reputation was established. Three great works fill the remainder of his life—three works often interrupted, carried on through a thousand hesitations, a thousand disappointments, quarrels with his patrons, quarrels with his family, quarrels perhaps most of all with himself—the Sistine Chapel, the Mausoleum of Julius the Second, and the Sacristy of *San Lorenzo*.

In the story of Michelangelo's life the strength, often turning to bitterness, is not far to seek. A discordant note sounds throughout it which almost spoils the music. He 'treats the Pope as the King of France himself would not dare to treat him:' he goes along the streets of Rome 'like an executioner,' Raphael says of him. Once he seems to have shut himself up with the intention of starving himself to death. As we come, in reading his life, on its harsh, untempered incidents, the thought again and again arises that he is one of those who incur the judgment of Dante, as having 'wilfully lived in sadness.' Even his tenderness and pity are embittered by their strength. What passionate weeping in that mysterious figure which, in the *Creation of Adam*, crouches below the image of the Almighty, as he comes with

the forms of things to be, woman and her progeny, in the
fold of his garment! What a sense of wrong in those two
captive youths, who feel the chains like scalding water on
their proud and delicate flesh! The idealist who became a
reformer with Savonarola, and a republican superintending
the fortification of Florence—the nest where he was born, *il
nido ove naqqu'io*, as he calls it once, in a sudden throb of
affection—in its last struggle for liberty, yet believed always
that he had imperial blood in his veins and was the kindred
of the great Matilda,* had within the depths of his nature
some secret spring of indignation or sorrow. We know little
of his youth, but all tends to make one believe in the
vehemence of its passions. Beneath the Platonic calm of the
sonnets there is latent a deep delight in carnal form and
colour. There, and still more in the madrigals, he often falls
into the language of less tranquil affections; while some of
them have the colour of penitence, as from a wanderer
returning home. He who spoke so decisively of the suprem-
acy in the imaginative world of the unveiled human form
had not been always, we may think, a mere Platonic lover.
Vague and wayward his loves may have been; but they
partook of the strength of his nature, and sometimes, it may
be, would by no means become music, so that the comely
order of his days was quite put out: *par che amaro ogni mio dolce
io senta.**

But his genius is in harmony with itself; and just as in the
products of his art we find resources of sweetness within their
exceeding strength, so in his own story also, bitter as the
ordinary sense of it may be, there are select pages shut in
among the rest—pages one might easily turn over too lightly,
but which yet sweeten the whole volume. The interest of
Michelangelo's poems is that they make us spectators of this
struggle; the struggle of a strong nature to adorn and attune
itself; the struggle of a desolating passion, which yearns to be
resigned and sweet and pensive, as Dante's was. It is a
consequence of the occasional and informal character of his
poetry, that it brings us nearer to himself, his own mind and
temper, than any work done only to support a literary
reputation could possibly do. His letters tell us little that is

worth knowing about him—a few poor quarrels about money and commissions. But it is quite otherwise with these songs and sonnets, written down at odd moments, sometimes on the margins of his sketches, themselves often unfinished sketches, arresting some salient feeling or unpremeditated idea as it passed. And it happens that a true study of these has become within the last few years for the first time possible. A few of the sonnets circulated widely in manuscript, and became almost within Michelangelo's own lifetime a subject of academical discourses. But they were first collected in a volume in 1623 by the great-nephew of Michelangelo, Michelangelo Buonarroti the younger. He omitted much, re-wrote the sonnets in part, and sometimes compressed two or more compositions into one, always losing something of the force and incisiveness of the original. So the book remained, neglected even by Italians themselves in the last century, through the influence of that French taste which despised all compositions of the kind, as it despised and neglected Dante. 'His reputation will ever be on the increase, because he is so little read,' says Voltaire of Dante.—But in 1858 the last of the Buonarroti bequeathed to the municipality of Florence the curiosities of his family. Among them was a precious volume containing the autograph of the sonnets. A learned Italian, Signor Cesare Guasti, undertook to collate this autograph with other manuscripts at the Vatican and elsewhere, and in 1863 published a true version of Michelangelo's poems, with dissertations and a paraphrase[1].

People have often spoken of these poems as if they were a mere cry of distress, a lover's complaint over the obduracy of Vittoria Colonna. But those who speak thus forget that though it is quite possible that Michelangelo had seen Vittoria, that somewhat shadowy figure, as early as 1537, yet their closer intimacy did not begin till about the year 1542, when Michelangelo was nearly seventy years old. Vittoria herself, an ardent neo-catholic, vowed to perpetual widowhood since the news had reached her, seventeen years before,

---

[1] The sonnets have been translated into English, with much skill, and poetic taste, by Mr. J. A. Symonds.

that her husband, the youthful and princely Marquess of Pescara, lay dead of the wounds he had received in the battle of Pavia, was then no longer an object of great passion. In a dialogue written by the painter, Francesco d'Ollanda, we catch a glimpse of them together in an empty church at Rome, one Sunday afternoon, discussing indeed the characteristics of various schools of art, but still more the writings of Saint Paul, already following the ways and tasting the sunless pleasures of weary people, whose care for external things is slackening. In a letter still extant he regrets that when he visited her after death he had kissed her hands only. He made, or set to work to make, a crucifix for her use, and two drawings, perhaps in preparation for it, are now in Oxford. From allusions in the sonnets, we may divine that when they first approached each other he had debated much with himself whether this last passion would be the most unsoftening, the most desolating of all—*un dolce amaro, un sì e no mi muovi.** Is it carnal affection, or, *del suo prestino stato* (of Plato's anti-natal state) *il raggio ardente?** The older, conventional criticism, dealing with the text of 1623, had lightly assumed that all or nearly all the sonnets were actually addressed to Vittoria herself; but Signor Guasti finds only four, or at most five, which can be so attributed on genuine authority. Still, there are reasons which make him assign the majority of them to the period between 1542 and 1547, and we may regard the volume as a record of this resting-place in Michelangelo's story. We know how Goethe escaped from the stress of sentiments too strong for him by making a book about them;* and for Michelangelo, to write down his passionate thoughts at all, to express them in a sonnet, was already in some measure to command, and have his way with them—

> *La vita del mia amor non è il cor mio,*
> *Ch'amor, di quel ch'io t'amo, è senza core.**

It was just because Vittoria raised no great passion that the space in his life where she reigns has such peculiar suavity; and the spirit of the sonnets is lost if we once take them out of that dreamy atmosphere in which men have things as they will, because the hold of all outward things upon them is faint and uncertain. Their prevailing tone is a calm and meditative sweetness. The cry of distress is indeed there, but as a mere residue, a trace of bracing chalybeate salt,* just discernible in the song which rises like a clear, sweet spring from a charmed space in his life.

This charmed and temperate space in Michelangelo's life, without which its excessive strength would have been so imperfect, which saves him from the judgment of Dante on those who 'wilfully lived in sadness,' is then a well-defined period there, reaching from the year 1542 to the year 1547, the year of Vittoria's death. In it the lifelong effort to tranquillise his vehement emotions by withdrawing them into the region of ideal sentiment, becomes successful; and the significance of Vittoria is, that she realises for him a type of affection which even in disappointment may charm and sweeten his spirit.

In this effort to tranquillise and sweeten life by idealising its vehement sentiments, there were two great traditional types, either of which an Italian of the sixteenth century might have followed. There was Dante, whose little book of the *Vita Nuova* had early become a pattern of imaginative love, maintained somewhat feebly by the later followers of Petrarch; and, since Plato had become something more than a name in Italy by the publication of the Latin translation of his works by Marsilio Ficino, there was the Platonic tradition also. Dante's belief in the resurrection of the body, through which, even in heaven, Beatrice loses for him no tinge of flesh-colour, or fold of raiment even; and the Platonic dream of the passage of the soul through one form of life after another, with its passionate haste to escape from the burden of bodily form altogether; are, for all effects of art or poetry, principles diametrically opposite. Now it is the Platonic tradition rather than Dante's that has moulded Michelangelo's verse. In many ways no sentiment could have been less like Dante's love for Beatrice than Michelangelo's for Vittoria Colonna. Dante's comes in early youth: Beatrice is a child, with the wistful, ambiguous vision of a child, with a character still unaccentuated by the influence of outward circumstances, almost expressionless. Vittoria, on the other hand, is a woman already weary, in advanced age, of grave intellectual qualities. Dante's story is a piece of figured work, inlaid with lovely incidents. In Michelangelo's poems, frost and fire are almost the only images—the refining fire of the goldsmith; once or twice the phœnix; ice melting at the fire; fire struck from the rock which it afterwards consumes. Except one doubtful allusion to a journey, there are almost no incidents. But there is much of the bright, sharp, unerring skill, with which in boyhood he gave the look of age to the head of a faun by chipping a tooth from its jaw with a single stroke of the hammer. For Dante, the amiable and devout materialism of the middle age sanctifies all that is presented by hand and eye; while Michelangelo is always pressing forward from the outward beauty—*il bel del fuor che agli occhi piace*,* to apprehend the unseen beauty; *transcenda nella forma universale**—that abstract form of beauty, about which the Platonists reason. And this gives the impression in him of something flitting and unfixed, of the houseless and complaining spirit, almost clairvoyant through the frail and yielding flesh. He accounts for love at first sight by a previous state of existence—*la dove io t'amai prima*.*

And yet there are many points in which he is really like Dante, and comes very near to the original image, beyond those later and feebler followers in the wake of Petrarch. He learns from Dante rather than from Plato, that for lovers, the surfeiting of desire—*ove gran desir gran copia affrena*, is a state less happy than poverty with abundance of hope—*una miseria di speranza piena*. He recalls him in the repetition of the words *gentile* and *cortesia*, in the personification of *Amor*, in the tendency to dwell minutely on the physical effects of the presence of a beloved object on the pulses and the heart. Above all, he resembles Dante in the warmth and intensity of his political utterances, for the lady of one of his noblest sonnets was from the first understood to be the city of Florence; and he avers that all must be asleep in heaven, if she, who was created 'of angelic form' for a thousand lovers, is appropriated by one alone, some Piero, or Alessandro de' Medici. Once and again he introduces Love and Death, who dispute concerning him. For, like Dante and all the nobler souls of Italy, he is much occupied with thoughts of the grave, and his true mistress is death,—death at first as the worst of all sorrows and disgraces, with a clod of the field for its brain; afterwards, death in its high distinction, its detachment from vulgar needs, the angry stains of life and action escaping fast.

Some of those whom the gods love die young. This man, because the gods loved him, lingered on to be of immense, patriarchal age, till the sweetness it had taken so long to secrete in him was found at last. Out of the strong come forth sweetness, *ex forti dulcedo.* The world had changed around him. The 'new catholicism' had taken the place of the Renaissance. The spirit of the Roman Church, had changed: in the vast world's cathedral which his skill had helped to raise for it, it looked stronger than ever. Some of the first members of the *Oratory** were among his intimate associates. They were of a spirit as unlike as possible from that of Lorenzo, or Savonarola even. The opposition of the Reformation to art has been often enlarged upon; far greater was that of the Catholic revival. But in thus fixing itself in a frozen orthodoxy, the Roman Church had passed beyond him, and he was a stranger to it. In earlier days, when its beliefs had been in a fluid state, he too might have been drawn into the controversy. He might have been for spiritualising the papal sovereignty, like Savonarola; or for adjusting the dreams of Plato and Homer with the words of Christ, like Pico of Mirandola. But things had moved onward, and such adjustments were no longer possible. For himself, he had long since fallen back on that divine ideal, which above the wear and tear of creeds has been forming itself for ages as the possession of nobler souls. And now he began to feel the soothing influence which since that time the Roman Church has often exerted over spirits too independent to be its subjects, yet brought within the neighbourhood of its action; consoled and tranquillised, as a traveller might be, resting for one evening in a strange city, by its stately aspect and the sentiment of its many fortunes, just because with those fortunes he has nothing to do. So he lingers on; a *revenant*, as the French say, a ghost out of another age, in a world too coarse to touch his faint sensibilities very closely; dreaming, in a worn-out society, theatrical in its life, theatrical in its art, theatrical even in its devotion, on the morning of the world's history, on the primitive form of man, on the images under which that primitive world had conceived of spiritual forces.

I have dwelt on the thought of Michelangelo as thus lingering beyond his time in a world not his own, because, if one is to distinguish the peculiar savour of his work, he must be approached, not through his followers, but through his predecessors; not through the marbles of *Saint Peter's*, but through the work of the sculptors of the fifteenth century over the tombs and altars of Tuscany. He is the last of the Florentines, of those on whom the peculiar sentiment of the Florence of Dante and Giotto descended: he is the consummate representative of the form that sentiment took in the fifteenth century with men like Luca Signorelli* and Mino da Fiesole.* Up to him the tradition of sentiment is unbroken, the progress towards surer and more mature methods of expressing that sentiment continuous. But his professed disciples did not share this temper; they are in love with his strength only, and seem not to feel his grave and temperate sweetness. Theatricality is their chief characteristic; and that is a quality as little attributable to Michelangelo as to Mino or Luca Signorelli. With him, as with them, all is serious, passionate, impulsive.

This discipleship of Michelangelo, this dependence of his on the tradition of the Florentine schools, is nowhere seen more clearly than in his treatment of the *Creation*. The *Creation of Man* had haunted the mind of the middle age like a dream; and weaving it into a hundred carved ornaments of capital or doorway, the Italian sculptors had early impressed upon it that pregnancy of expression which seems to give it many veiled meanings. As with other artistic conceptions of the middle age, its treatment became almost conventional, handed on from artist to artist, with slight changes, till it came to have almost an independent and abstract existence of its own. It was characteristic of the medieval mind thus to give an independent traditional existence to a special pictorial conception, or to a legend, like that of *Tristram* or *Tannhäuser*, or even to the very thoughts and substance of a book, like the *Imitation*, so that no single workman could claim it as his own, and the book, the image, the legend, had itself a legend, and its fortunes, and a personal history; and it is a sign of the medievalism of Michelangelo, that he thus receives from tradition his central conception, and does but add the last touches, in transferring it to the frescoes of the Sistine Chapel.

But there was another tradition of those earlier, more serious Florentines, of which Michelangelo is the inheritor, to which he gives the final expression, and which centres in the sacristy of *San Lorenzo*, as the tradition of the *Creation* centres in the Sistine Chapel. It has been said that all the great Florentines were preoccupied with death. *Outre-tombe! Outre-tombe!*—is the burden of their thoughts, from Dante to Savonarola. Even the gay and licentious Boccaccio gives a keener edge to his stories by putting them in the mouths of a party of people who had taken refuge in a country-house from the danger of death by plague. It was to this inherited sentiment, this practical decision that to be preoccupied with the thought of death was in itself dignifying, and a note of high quality, that the seriousness of the great Florentines of the fifteenth century was partly due; and it was reinforced in them by the actual sorrows of their times. How often, and in what various ways, had they seen life stricken down, in their streets and houses. *La bella Simonetta* dies in early youth, and is borne to the grave with uncovered face. The young Cardinal Jacopo di Portogallo* dies on a visit to Florence— *insignis formâ fui et mirabili modestiâ*—his epitaph dares to say. Antonio Rossellino carves his tomb in the church of San Miniato, with care for the shapely hands and feet, and sacred attire; Luca della Robbia puts his skyiest works there; and the tomb of the youthful and princely prelate became the strangest and most beautiful thing in that strange and beautiful place. After the execution of the Pazzi conspirators,* Botticelli is employed to paint their portraits. This preoccupation with serious thoughts and sad images might easily have resulted, as it did, for instance, in the gloomy villages of the Rhine, or in the overcrowded parts of medieval Paris, as it still does in many a village of the Alps, in something merely morbid or grotesque, in the *Danse Macabre* of many French and German painters, or the grim inventions of Dürer. From such a result the Florentine masters of the fifteenth century were saved by the nobility of their Italian culture, and still more by their tender pity for the thing itself. They must often have leaned over the lifeless body, when all was at length quiet and smoothed out. After death, it is said, the traces of slighter and more superficial dispositions disappear; the lines become more simple and dignified; only the abstract lines remain, in a great indifference. They came thus to see death in its distinction. Then following it perhaps one stage further, dwelling for a moment on the point where all this transitory dignity must break up, and discerning with no clearness a new body, they paused just in time, and abstained, with a sentiment of profound pity.

Of all this sentiment Michelangelo is the achievement; and, first of all, of pity. *Pietà*, pity, the pity of the Virgin Mother over the dead body of Christ, expanded into the pity of all mothers over all dead sons, the entombment, with its cruel 'hard stones':—this is the subject of his predilection. He has left it in many forms, sketches, half-finished designs, finished and unfinished groups of sculpture; but always as a hopeless, rayless, almost heathen sorrow—no divine sorrow, but mere pity and awe at the stiff limbs and colourless lips. There is a drawing of his at Oxford,* in which the dead body has sunk to the earth between the mother's feet, with the arms extended over her knees. The tombs in the sacristy of *San Lorenzo* are memorials, not of any of the nobler and greater Medici, but of Giuliano, and Lorenzo the younger, noticeable chiefly for their somewhat early death. It is mere human nature therefore which has prompted the sentiment here. The titles assigned traditionally to the four symbolical figures, *Night* and *Day*, *The Twilight* and *The Dawn*, are far too definite for them; for these figures come much nearer to the mind and spirit of their author, and are a more direct expression of his thoughts, than any merely symbolical conceptions could possibly have been. They concentrate and express, less by way of definite conceptions than by the touches, the promptings of a piece of music, all those vague fancies, misgivings, presentiments, which shift and mix and are defined and fade again, whenever the thoughts try to fix themselves with sincerity on the conditions and surroundings of the disembodied spirit. I suppose no one would come to the sacristy of San Lorenzo for consolation; for seriousness, for solemnity, for dignity of impression, perhaps, but not for consolation. It is a place neither of consoling nor of terrible thoughts, but of vague and wistful speculation. Here, again, Michelangelo is the disciple not so much of Dante as of the Platonists. Dante's belief in immortality is formal, precise, and firm, almost as much so as that of a child, who thinks the dead will hear if you cry loud enough. But in Michelangelo you have maturity, the mind of the grown man, dealing cautiously and dispassionately with serious things; and what hope he has is based on the consciousness of ignorance— ignorance of man, ignorance of the nature of the mind, its origin and capacities. Michelangelo is so ignorant of the spiritual world, of the new body and its laws, that he does not surely know whether the consecrated Host may not be the body of Christ. And of all that range of sentiment he is the poet, a poet still alive, and in possession of our inmost thoughts—dumb inquiry over the relapse after death into the formlessness which preceded life, the change, the revolt from that change, then the correcting, hallowing, consoling rush of pity; at last, far off, thin and vague, yet not more vague than the most definite thoughts men have had through three centuries on a matter that has been so near their hearts, the new body—a passing light, a mere intangible, external effect, over those too rigid, or too formless faces; a dream that lingers a moment, retreating in the dawn, incomplete, aimless, helpless; a thing with faint hearing, faint memory, faint power of touch; a breath, a flame in the doorway, a feather in the wind.

The qualities of the great masters in art or literature, the

combination of those qualities, the laws by which they
moderate, support, relieve each other, are not peculiar to
them; but most often typical standards, or revealing instances of the laws by which certain æsthetic effects are
produced. The old masters indeed are simpler; their characteristics are written larger, and are easier to read, than the
analogues of them in all the mixed, confused productions of
the modern mind. But when once we have succeeded in
defining for ourselves those characteristics, and the law of
their combination, we have acquired a standard or measure
which helps us to put in its right place many a vagrant
genius, many an unclassified talent, many precious though
imperfect products of art. It is so with the components of the
true character of Michelangelo. That strange interfusion of
sweetness and strength is not to be found in those who
claimed to be his followers; but it is found in many of those
who worked before him, and in many others down to our
own time, in William Blake, for instance, and Victor Hugo,
who, though not of his school, and unaware, are his true
sons, and help us to understand him, as he in turn interprets
and justifies them. Perhaps this is the chief use in studying
old masters.

1871.

LEONARDO DA VINCI

[*HOMO MINISTER ET INTERPRES NATURÆ*]*

IN Vasari's life of Leonardo da Vinci as we now read it there are some variations from the first edition. There, the painter who has fixed the outward type of Christ for succeeding centuries was a bold speculator, holding lightly by other men's beliefs, setting philosophy above Christianity. Words of his, trenchant enough to justify this impression, are not recorded, and would have been out of keeping with a genius of which one characteristic is the tendency to lose itself in a refined and graceful mystery. The suspicion was but the time-honoured mode in which the world stamps its appreciation of one who has thoughts for himself alone, his high indifference, his intolerance of the common forms of things; and in the second edition the image was changed into something fainter and more conventional. But it is still by a certain mystery in his work, and something enigmatical beyond the usual measure of great men, that he fascinates, or perhaps half repels. His life is one of sudden revolts, with intervals in which he works not at all, or apart from the main scope of his work. By a strange fortune the pictures on which his more popular fame rested disappeared early from the world, like the *Battle of the Standard*; or are mixed obscurely with the product of meaner hands, like the *Last Supper*.* His type of beauty is so exotic that it fascinates a larger number than it delights, and seems more than that of any other artist to reflect ideas and views and some scheme of the world within; so that he seemed to his contemporaries to be the possessor of some unsanctified and secret wisdom; as to Michelet and others to have anticipated modern ideas. He trifles with his genius, and crowds all his chief work into a few tormented years of later life; yet he is so possessed by his genius that he passes unmoved through the most tragic events, overwhelming his country and friends, like one who comes across them by chance on some secret errand.

His *legend*, as the French say, with the anecdotes which every one remembers, is one of the most brilliant chapters of Vasari. Later writers merely copied it, until, in 1804, Carlo Amoretti* applied to it a criticism which left hardly a date fixed, and not one of those anecdotes untouched. The various questions thus raised have since that time become, one after another, subjects of special study, and mere antiquarianism has in this direction little more to do. For others remain the editing of the thirteen books of his manuscripts, and the separation by technical criticism of what in his reputed works is really his, from what is only half his, or the work of his pupils. But a lover of strange souls may still analyse for himself the impression made on him by those works, and try to reach through it a definition of the chief elements of Leonardo's genius. The *legend*, as corrected and enlarged by its critics, may now and then intervene to support the results of this analysis.

His life has three divisions—thirty years at Florence, nearly twenty years at Milan, then nineteen years of wandering, till he sinks to rest under the protection of Francis the First at the *Château de Clou*. The dishonour of illegitimacy hangs over his birth. Piero Antonio, his father, was of a noble Florentine house, of Vinci in the *Val d'Arno*, and Leonardo, brought up delicately among the true children of that house, was the love-child of his youth, with the keen, puissant nature such children often have. We see him in his boyhood fascinating all men by his beauty, improvising music and songs, buying the caged birds and setting them free, as he walked the streets of Florence, fond of odd bright dresses and spirited horses.

From his earliest years he designed many objects, and constructed models in relief, of which Vasari mentions some of women smiling. His father, pondering over this promise in the child, took him to the workshop of Andrea del Verrocchio,* then the most famous artist in Florence. Beautiful objects lay about there—reliquaries, pyxes, silver images for the pope's chapel at Rome, strange fancy-work of the middle age, keeping odd company with fragments of antiquity, then but lately discovered. Another student Leonardo may have seen there—a lad into whose soul the level light and aerial illusions of Italian sunsets had passed, in after days famous as Perugino. Verrocchio was an artist of the earlier Florentine type, carver, painter, and worker in metals, in one; designer, not of pictures only, but of all things for sacred or household use, drinking-vessels, ambries, instruments of music, making them all fair to look upon, filling the common ways of life with the reflexion of some far-off brightness; and years of patience had refined his hand till his work was now sought after from distant places.

It happened that Verrocchio was employed by the brethren of Vallombrosa to paint the Baptism of Christ, and Leonardo was allowed to finish an angel in the left-hand corner. It was one of those moments in which the progress of a great thing—here, that of the art of Italy—presses hard on the happiness of an individual, through whose discouragement and decrease, humanity, in more fortunate persons, comes a step nearer to its final success.

For beneath the cheerful exterior of the mere well-paid craftsman, chasing brooches for the copes of *Santa Maria Novella*, or twisting metal screens for the tombs of the Medici, lay the ambitious desire to expand the destiny of Italian art by a larger knowledge and insight into things, a purpose in art not unlike Leonardo's still unconscious purpose; and often, in the modelling of drapery, or of a lifted arm, or of hair cast back from the face, there came to him something of the freer manner and richer humanity of a later age. But in this *Baptism* the pupil had surpassed the master; and Verrocchio turned away as one stunned, and as if his sweet earlier work must thereafter be distasteful to him, from the bright animated angel of Leonardo's hand.

The angel may still be seen in Florence, a space of sunlight in the cold, laboured old picture; but the legend is true only in sentiment, for painting had always been the art by which Verrocchio set least store. And as in a sense he anticipates Leonardo, so, to the last Leonardo recalls the studio of Verrocchio, in the love of beautiful toys, such as the vessel of water for a mirror, and lovely needlework about the implicated hands in the *Modesty and Vanity*, and of reliefs, like those cameos which in the *Virgin of the Balances* hang all round the girdle of Saint Michael, and of bright variegated stones, such as the agates in the *Saint Anne*,* and in a hieratic preciseness and grace, as of a sanctuary swept and garnished. Amid all the cunning and intricacy of his Lombard manner this never left him. Much of it there must have been in that lost picture of *Paradise*, which he prepared as a cartoon for tapestry, to be woven in the looms of Flanders. It was the perfection of the older Florentine style of miniature-painting, with patient putting of each leaf upon the trees and each flower in the grass, where the first man and woman were standing.

And because it was the perfection of that style, it awoke in Leonardo some seed of discontent which lay in the secret places of his nature. For the way to perfection is through a series of disgusts; and this picture—all that he had done so far in his life at Florence—was after all in the old slight manner. His art, if it was to be something in the world, must be weighted with more of the meaning of nature and purpose of humanity. Nature was 'the true mistress of higher intelligences.' He plunged, then, into the study of nature. And in doing this he followed the manner of the older students; he brooded over the hidden virtues of plants and crystals, the lines traced by the stars as they moved in the sky, over the correspondences which exist between the different orders of living things, through which, to eyes opened, they interpret each other; and for years he seemed to those about him as one listening to a voice, silent for other men.

He learned here the art of going deep, of tracking the sources of expression to their subtlest retreats, the power of an intimate presence in the things he handled. He did not at once or entirely desert his art; only he was no longer the cheerful, objective painter, through whose soul, as through clear glass, the bright figures of Florentine life, only made a little mellower and more pensive by the transit, passed on to the white wall. He wasted many days in curious tricks of design, seeming to lose himself in the spinning of intricate devices of line and colour. He was smitten with a love of the impossible—the perforation of mountains, changing the course of rivers, raising great buildings, such as the church of *San Giovanni*, in the air; all those feats for the performance of which natural magic professed to have the key. Later writers, indeed, see in these efforts an anticipation of modern mechanics; in him they were rather dreams, thrown off by the overwrought and labouring brain. Two ideas were especially confirmed in him, as reflexes of things that had touched his brain in childhood beyond the depth of other impressions—the smiling of women and the motion of great waters.

And in such studies some interfusion of the extremes of beauty and terror shaped itself, as an image that might be seen and touched, in the mind of this gracious youth, so fixed that for the rest of his life it never left him. As if catching glimpses of it in the strange eyes or hair of chance people, he would follow such about the streets of Florence till the sun went down, of whom many sketches of his remain. Some of these are full of a curious beauty, that remote beauty which may be apprehended only by those who have sought it carefully; who, starting with acknowledged types of beauty, have refined as far upon these, as these refine upon the world of common forms. But mingled inextricably with this there is an element of mockery also; so that, whether in sorrow or scorn, he caricatures Dante even. Legions of grotesques sweep under his hand; for has not nature too her grotesques—the rent rock, the distorting lights of evening on lonely roads, the unveiled structure of man in the embryo, or the skeleton?

All these swarming fancies unite in the *Medusa* of the *Uffizii*. Vasari's story* of an earlier Medusa, painted on a wooden shield, is perhaps an invention; and yet, properly told, has more of the air of truth about it than anything else in the whole legend. For its real subject is not the serious work of a man, but the experiment of a child. The lizards and glow-worms and other strange small creatures which haunt an Italian vineyard bring before one the whole picture of a child's life in a Tuscan dwelling—half castle, half farm—and are as true to nature as the pretended astonishment of the father for whom the boy has prepared a surprise.

It was not in play that he painted that other Medusa, the one great picture which he left behind him in Florence. The subject has been treated in various ways; Leonardo alone cuts to its centre; he alone realises it as the head of a corpse, exercising its powers through all the circumstances of death. What may be called the fascination of corruption penetrates in every touch its exquisitely finished beauty. About the dainty lines of the cheek the bat flits unheeded. The delicate snakes seem literally strangling each other in terrified struggle to escape from the Medusa brain. The hue which violent death always brings with it is in the features; features singularly massive and grand, as we catch them inverted, in a dexterous foreshortening, crown foremost, like a great calm stone against which the wave of serpents breaks.

The science of that age was all divination, clairvoyance, unsubjected to our exact modern formulas, seeking in an instant of vision to concentrate a thousand experiences. Later writers, thinking only of the well-ordered treatise* on painting which a Frenchman, Raffaelle du Fresne, a hundred years afterwards, compiled from Leonardo's bewildered manuscripts, written strangely, as his manner was, from right to left, have imagined a rigid order in his inquiries. But this rigid order would have been little in accordance with the restlessness of his character; and if we think of him as the mere reasoner who subjects design to anatomy, and composition to mathematical rules, we shall hardly have that impression which those around Leonardo received from him. Poring over his crucibles, making experiments with colour, trying, by a strange variation of the alchemist's dream, to discover the secret, not of an elixir to make man's natural life immortal, but of giving immortality to the subtlest and most delicate effects of painting, he seemed to them rather the sorcerer or the magician, possessed of curious secrets and a hidden knowledge, living in a world of which he alone possessed the key. What his philosophy seems to have been most like is that of Paracelsus or Cardan;* and much of the spirit of the older alchemy still hangs about it, with its confidence in short cuts and odd byways to knowledge. To him philosophy was to be something giving strange swiftness and double sight, divining the sources of springs beneath the earth or of expression beneath the human countenance, clairvoyant of occult gifts in common or uncommon things, in the reed at the brook-side, or the star which draws near to us but once in a century. How, in this way, the clear purpose was overclouded, the fine chaser's hand perplexed, we but dimly see; the mystery which at no point quite lifts from Leonardo's life is deepest here. But it is certain that at one period of his life he had almost ceased to be an artist.

The year 1483—the year of the birth of Raphael and the thirty-first of Leonardo's life—is fixed as the date of his visit to Milan by the letter in which he recommends himself to Ludovico Sforza,* and offers to tell him, for a price, strange secrets in the art of war. It was that Sforza who murdered his his young nephew by slow poison, yet was so susceptible of religious impressions that he blended mere earthly passion with a sort of religious sentimentalism, and who took for his device the mulberry-tree—symbol, in its long delay and sudden yielding of flowers and fruit together, of a wisdom which economises all forces for an opportunity of sudden and sure effect. The fame of Leonardo had gone before him, and he was to model a colossal statue of Francesco, the first Duke of Milan. As for Leonardo himself, he came not as an artist at all, or careful of the fame of one; but as a player on the harp, a strange harp of silver of his own construction, shaped in some curious likeness to a horse's skull. The capricious spirit of Ludovico was susceptible also to the power of music, and Leonardo's nature had a kind of spell in it. Fascination is always the word descriptive of him. No portrait of his youth remains; but all tends to make us believe that up to this time some charm of voice and aspect, strong enough to balance the disadvantage of his birth, had played about him. His physical strength was great; it was said that he could bend a horse-shoe like a coil of lead.

The *Duomo*,* work of artists from beyond the Alps, so fantastic to the eye of a Florentine used to the mellow, unbroken surfaces of Giotto and Arnolfo, was then in all its freshness; and below, in the streets of Milan, moved a people as fantastic, changeful, and dreamlike. To Leonardo least of all men could there be anything poisonous in the exotic flowers of sentiment which grew there. It was a life of brilliant sins and exquisite amusements: Leonardo became a celebrated designer of pageants; and it suited the quality of his genius, composed, in almost equal parts, of curiosity and the desire of beauty, to take things as they came.

Curiosity and the desire of beauty—these are the two elementary forces in Leonardo's genius; curiosity often in conflict with the desire of beauty, but generating, in union with it, a type of subtle and curious grace.

The movement of the fifteenth century was two-fold; partly the Renaissance, partly also the coming of what is called the 'modern spirit,' with its realism, its appeal to experience. It comprehended a return to antiquity, and a return to nature. Raphael represents the return to antiquity, and Leonardo the return to nature. In this return to nature, he was seeking to satisfy a boundless curiosity by her perpetual surprises, a microscopic sense of finish by her *finesse*, or delicacy of operation, that *subtilitas naturae** which Bacon notices. So we find him often in intimate relations with men of science,—with Fra Luca Paccioli the mathematician, and the anatomist Marc Antonio della Torre. His observations and experiments fill thirteen volumes of manuscript; and those who can judge describe him as anticipating long before, by rapid intuition, the later ideas of science. He explained the obscure light of the unilluminated part of the moon, knew that the sea had once covered the mountains which contain shells, and of the gathering of the equatorial waters above the polar.

He who thus penetrated into the most secret parts of nature preferred always the more to the less remote, what, seeming exceptional, was an instance of law more refined, the construction about things of a peculiar atmosphere and mixed lights. He paints flowers with such curious felicity that different writers have attributed to him a fondness for particular flowers, as Clement the cyclamen, and Rio the jasmin; while, at Venice, there is a stray leaf from his portfolio dotted all over with studies of violets and the wild rose. In him first appears the taste for what is *bizarre* or *recherché* in landscape; hollow places full of the green shadow of bituminous rocks, ridged reefs of trap-rock which cut the water into quaint sheets of light,—their exact antitype is in our own western seas; all the solemn effects of moving water. You may follow it springing from its distant source among the rocks on the heath of the *Madonna of the Balances*, passing, as a little fall, into the treacherous calm of the *Madonna of the Lake*, as a goodly river next, below the cliffs of the *Madonna of the Rocks*, washing the white walls of its distant villages, stealing out in a network of divided streams in *La Gioconda* to the seashore of the *Saint Anne*—that delicate place, where the wind passes like the point of some fine etcher over the surface, and the untorn shells are lying thick upon the sand, and the tops of the rocks, to which the waves never rise, are green with grass, grown fine as hair. It is the landscape, not of dreams or of fancy, but of places far withdrawn, and hours selected from a thousand with a miracle of *finesse*. Through Leonardo's strange veil of sight things reach him so; in no ordinary night or day, but as in faint light of eclipse, or in some brief interval of falling rain at daybreak, or through deep water.

And not into nature only; but he plunged also into human personality, and became above all a painter of portraits; faces of a modelling more skilful than has been seen before or since, embodied with a reality which almost amounts to illusion, on the dark air. To take a character as it was, and delicately sound its stops, suited one so curious in observation, curious in invention. He painted thus the portraits of Ludovico's mistresses, Lucretia Crivelli and Cecilia Galerani the poetess, of Ludovico himself, and the Duchess Beatrice. The portrait of Cecilia Galerani is lost, but that of Lucretia Crivelli has been identified with *La Belle Feronière* of the Louvre, and Ludovico's pale, anxious face still remains in the Ambrosian library. Opposite is the portrait of Beatrice d'Este, in whom Leonardo seems to have caught some presentiment of early death, painting her precise and grave, full of the refinement of the dead, in sad earth-coloured raiment, set with pale stones.

Sometimes this curiosity came in conflict with the desire of beauty; it tended to make him go too far below that outside of things in which art really begins and ends. This struggle between the reason and its ideas, and the senses, the desire of beauty, is the key to Leonardo's life at Milan—his restlessness, his endless re-touchings, his odd experiments with colour. How much must he leave unfinished, how much recommence! His problem was the transmutation of ideas into images. What he had attained so far had been the mastery of that earlier Florentine style, with its naïve and limited sensuousness. Now he was to entertain in this narrow medium those divinations of a humanity too wide for it, that larger vision of the opening world, which is only not too much for the great, irregular art of Shakespeare; and everywhere the effort is visible in the work of his hands. This agitation, this perpetual delay, give him an air of weariness and *ennui*. To others he seems to be aiming at an impossible effect, to do something that art, that painting, can never do. Often the expression of physical beauty at this or that point seems strained and marred in the effort, as in those heavy German foreheads—too heavy and German for perfect beauty.

For there was a touch of Germany in that genius which, as Goethe said, had 'thought itself weary'—*müde sich gedacht*. What an anticipation of modern Germany, for instance, in that debate on the question whether sculpture or painting is the nobler art[1]! But there is this difference between him and the German, that, with all that curious science, the German would have thought nothing more was needed. The name of Goethe himself reminds one how great for the artist may be the danger of over-much science; how Goethe, who, in the *Elective Affinities* and the first part of *Faust*, does transmute ideas into images, who wrought many such transmutations, did not invariably find the spell-word, and in the second part of *Faust* presents us with a mass of science which has almost no artistic character at all. But Leonardo will never work till

---

[1] How princely, how characteristic of Leonardo, the answer, *Quanto più un' arte porta seco fatica di corpo tanto più è vile!**

the happy moment comes—that moment of *bien-être*,* which to imaginative men is the moment of invention. On this he waits with a perfect patience; other moments are but a preparation, or after-taste of it. Few men distinguish between them as jealously as he. Hence, so many flaws even in the choicest work. But for Leonardo the distinction is absolute, and, in the moment of *bien-être*, the alchemy complete: the idea is stricken into colour and imagery: a cloudy mysticism is refined to a subdued and graceful mystery, and painting pleases the eye while it satisfies the soul.

This curious beauty is seen above all in his drawings, and in these chiefly in the abstract grace of the bounding lines. Let us take some of these drawings,* and pause over them awhile; and, first, one of those at Florence—the heads of a woman and a little child, set side by side, but each in its own separate frame. First of all, there is much pathos in the reappearance, in the fuller curves of the face of the child, of the sharper, more chastened lines of the worn and older face, which leaves no doubt that the heads are those of a little child and its mother. A feeling for maternity is indeed always characteristic of Leonardo; and this feeling is further indicated here by the half-humorous pathos of the diminutive, rounded shoulders of the child. You may note a like pathetic power in drawings of a young man, seated in a stooping posture, his face in his hands, as in sorrow; of a slave sitting in an uneasy inclined attitude, in some brief interval of rest; of a small Madonna and Child, peeping sideways in half-reassured terror, as a mighty griffin with batlike wings, one of Leonardo's finest *inventions*, descends suddenly from the air to snatch up a great wild beast wandering near them. But note in these, as that which especially belongs to art, the contour of the young man's hair, the poise of the slave's arm above his head, and the curves of the head of the child, following the little skull within, thin and fine as some sea-shell worn by the wind.

Take again another head, still more full of sentiment, but of a different kind, a little drawing in red chalk which every one will remember who has examined at all carefully the drawings by old masters at the Louvre. It is a face of doubtful sex, set in the shadow of its own hair, the cheek-line in high light against it, with something voluptuous and full in the eyelids and the lips. Another drawing might pass for the same face in childhood, with parched and feverish lips, but much sweetness in the loose, short-waisted childish dress, with necklace and *bulla*, and in the daintily bound hair. We might take the thread of suggestion which these two drawings offer, when thus set side by side, and, following it through the drawings at Florence, Venice, and Milan, construct a sort of series, illustrating better than anything else Leonardo's type of womanly beauty. Daughters of Herodias,* with their fantastic head-dresses knotted and folded so strangely to leave the dainty oval of the face disengaged, they are not of the Christian family, or of Raphael's. They are the clairvoyants, through whom, as through delicate instruments, one becomes aware of the subtler forces of nature, and the modes of their action, all that is magnetic in it, all those finer conditions wherein material things rise to that subtlety of operation which constitutes them spiritual, where only the finer nerve and the keener touch can follow. It is as if in certain significant examples we actually saw those forces at their work on human flesh. Nervous, electric, faint always with some inexplicable faintness, these people seem to be subject to exceptional conditions, to feel powers at work in the common air unfelt by others, to become, as it were, the receptacle of them, and pass them on to us in a chain of secret influences.

But among the more youthful heads there is one at Florence which Love chooses for its own—the head of a young man,* which may well be the likeness of Andréa Salaino, beloved of Leonardo for his curled and waving hair—*belli capelli ricci e inanellati*—and afterwards his favourite pupil and servant. Of all the interests in living men and women which may have filled his life at Milan, this attachment alone is recorded. And in return Salaino identified himself so entirely with Leonardo, that the picture of *St. Anne*, in the Louvre, has been attributed to him. It illustrates Leonardo's usual choice of pupils, men of some natural charm of person or intercourse like Salaino, or men of birth and princely habits of life like Francesco Melzi*— men with just enough genius to be capable of initiation into his secret, for the sake of which they were ready to efface their own individuality. Among them, retiring often to the villa of the Melzi at *Canonica al Vaprio*, he worked at his fugitive manuscripts and sketches, working for the present hour, and for a few only, perhaps chiefly for himself. Other artists have been as careless of present or future applause, in self-forgetfulness, or because they set moral or political ends above the ends of art; but in him this solitary culture of beauty seems to have hung upon a kind of self-love, and a carelessness in the work of art of all but art itself. Out of the secret places of a unique temperament he brought strange blossoms and fruits hitherto unknown; and for him, the novel impression conveyed, the exquisite effect woven, counted as an end in itself—a perfect end.

And these pupils of his acquired his manner so thoroughly, that though the number of Leonardo's authentic works is very small indeed, there is a multitude of other men's pictures through which we undoubtedly see him, and come very near to his genius. Sometimes, as in the little picture of the *Madonna of the Balances*, in which, from the bosom of His mother, Christ weighs the pebbles of the brook against the sins of men, we have a hand, rough enough by contrast, working upon some fine hint or sketch of his. Sometimes, as in the subjects of the *Daughter of Herodias* and the *Head of John the Baptist*, the lost originals have been re-echoed and varied upon again and again by Luini* and others. At other times the original remains, but has been a mere theme or motive, a type of which the accessories might be modified or changed; and these variations have but brought out the more the purpose, or expression of the original. It is so with the so-called *Saint John the Baptist* of the Louvre—one of the few naked figures Leonardo painted—whose delicate brown flesh and woman's hair no one would go out into the wilderness to seek, and whose treacherous smile would have us understand something far beyond the outward gesture or circumstance. But the long, reedlike cross in the hand, which suggests Saint John the Baptist, becomes faint in a copy at the Ambrosian Library, and disappears altogether in another version, in the *Palazzo Rosso* at Genoa. Returning from the latter to the original, we are no longer surprised by Saint John's strange likeness to the *Bacchus* which hangs near it, and which set Théophile Gautier* thinking of Heine's notion of decayed gods, who, to maintain themselves, after the fall of paganism, took employment in the new religion. We recognise one of those symbolical inventions in which the ostensible subject is used, not as matter for definite pictorial realisation, but as the starting-point of a train of sentiment, subtle and vague as a piece of music. No one ever ruled over the mere *subject* in hand more entirely than Leonardo, or bent it more dexterously to purely artistic ends. And so it comes to pass that though he handles sacred subjects continually, he is the most profane of painters; the given person or subject, Saint John in the Desert, or the Virgin on the knees of Saint Anne, is often merely the pretext for a kind of work which carried one altogether beyond the range of its conventional associations.

About the *Last Supper*, its decay and restorations, a whole literature has risen up, Goethe's pensive sketch* of its sad fortunes being perhaps the best. The death in child-birth of the Duchess Beatrice was followed in Ludovico by one of those paroxysms of religious feeling which in him were constitutional. The low, gloomy Dominican church of *Saint Mary of the Graces* had been the favourite oratory of Beatrice. She had spent her last days there, full of sinister presentiments; at last it had been almost necessary to remove her from it by force; and now it was here that mass was said a hundred times a day for her repose. On the damp wall of the refectory, oozing with mineral salts, Leonardo painted the *Last Supper*. Effective anecdotes were told about it, his retouchings and delays. They show him refusing to work except at the moment of invention, scornful of anyone who supposed that art could be a work of mere industry and rule, often coming the whole length of Milan to give a single touch. He painted it, not in fresco, where all must be *impromptu*, but in oils, the new method which he had been one of the first to welcome, because it allowed of so many after-thoughts, so refined a working-out of perfection. It turned out that on a plastered wall no process could have been less durable. Within fifty years it had fallen into decay. And now we have to turn back to Leonardo's own studies, above all to one drawing of the central head at the *Brera*,* which, in a union of tenderness and severity in the face-lines, reminds one of the monumental work of Mino da Fiesole, to trace it as it was.

Here was another effort to lift a given subject out of the range of its traditional associations. Strange, after all the mystic developments of the middle age, was the effort to see the Eucharist, not as the pale Host of the altar, but as one taking leave of his friends. Five years afterwards the young Raphael, at Florence, painted it with sweet and solemn effect in the refectory of Saint Onofrio; but still with all the mystical unreality of the school of Perugino. Vasari pretends that the central head was never finished. But finished or unfinished, or owing part of its effect to a mellowing decay, the head of Jesus does but consummate the sentiment of the whole company—ghosts through which you see the wall, faint as the shadows of the leaves upon the wall on autumn afternoons. This figure is but the faintest, the most spectral of them all.

The *Last Supper* was finished in 1497; in 1498 the French entered Milan, and whether or not the Gascon bowmen used it as a mark for their arrows, the model of Francesco Sforza certainly did not survive. What, in that age, such work was capable of being—of what nobility, amid what racy truth-fulness to fact—we may judge from the bronze statue of Bartolomeo Colleoni on horseback, modelled by Leonardo's master, Verrocchio, (he died of grief, it was said, because, the mould accidentally failing, he was unable to complete it,) still standing in the *piazza* of Saint John and Saint Paul at Venice. Some traces of the thing may remain in certain of Leonardo's drawings, and perhaps also, by a singular cir-cumstance, in a far-off town of France. For Ludovico became a prisoner, and ended his days at Loches in

Touraine. After many years of captivity in the dungeons
below, where all seems sick with barbarous feudal memories,
he was allowed at last, it is said, to breathe fresher air for
awhile in one of the rooms of the great tower still shown, its
walls covered with strange painted arabesques, ascribed by
tradition to his hand, amused a little, in this way, through
the tedious years. In those vast helmets and human faces and
pieces of armour, among which, in great letters, the motto
*Infelix Sum** is woven in and out, it is perhaps not too fanciful
to see the fruit of a wistful after-dreaming over Leonardo's
sundry experiments on the armed figure of the great duke,
which had occupied the two so much during the days of their
good fortune at Milan.

The remaining years of Leonardo's life are more or less
years of wandering. From his brilliant life at court he had
saved nothing, and he returned to Florence a poor man.
Perhaps necessity kept his spirit excited: the next four years
are one prolonged rapture or ecstasy of invention. He
painted now the pictures of the Louvre, his most authentic
works, which came there straight from the cabinet of Francis
the First, at Fontainebleau. One picture of his, the *Saint
Anne*—not the *Saint Anne* of the Louvre, but a simple cartoon,
now in London—revived for a moment a sort of appreciation more common in an earlier time, when good pictures
had still seemed miraculous. For two days a crowd of people
of all qualities passed in naïve excitement through the
chamber where it hung, and gave Leonardo a taste of the
'triumph' of Cimabue.* But his work was less with the saints
than with the living women of Florence. For he lived still in
the polished society that he loved, and in the houses of
Florence, left perhaps a little subject to light thoughts by the
death of Savonarola—the latest gossip (1869) is of an
undraped Monna Lisa, found in some out-of-the-way corner
of the late *Orleans* collection—he saw Ginevra di Benci, and
Lisa, the young third wife of Francesco del Giocondo. As we
have seen him using incidents of sacred story, not for their
own sake, or as mere subjects for pictorial realisation, but as
a cryptic language for fancies all his own, so now he found a
vent for his thought in taking one of these languid women,

and raising her, as Leda or Pomona, as Modesty or Vanity, to the seventh heaven of symbolical expression.

La Gioconda is, in the truest sense, Leonardo's masterpiece, the revealing instance of his mode of thought and work. In suggestiveness, only the *Melancholia* of Dürer is comparable to it; and no crude symbolism disturbs the effect of its subdued and graceful mystery. We all know the face and hands of the figure, set in its marble chair, in that circle of fantastic rocks, as in some faint light under sea. Perhaps of all ancient pictures time has chilled it least[1]. As often happens with works in which invention seems to reach its limit, there is an element in it given to, not invented by, the master. In that inestimable folio of drawings, once in the possession of Vasari, were certain designs by Verrocchio, faces of such impressive beauty that Leonardo in his boyhood copied them many times. It is hard not to connect with these designs of the elder, by-past master, as with its germinal principle, the unfathomable smile, always with a touch of something sinister in it, which plays over all Leonardo's work. Besides, the picture is a portrait. From childhood we see this image defining itself on the fabric of his dreams; and but for express historical testimony, we might fancy that this was but his ideal lady, embodied and beheld at last. What was the relationship of a living Florentine to this creature of his thought? By what strange affinities had the dream and the person grown up thus apart, and yet so closely together? Present from the first incorporeally in Leonardo's brain, dimly traced in the designs of Verrocchio, she is found present at last in *Il Giocondo's* house. That there is much of mere portraiture in the picture is attested by the legend that by artificial means, the presence of mimes and flute-players, that subtle expression was protracted on the face. Again, was it in four years and by renewed labour never really completed, or in four months and as by stroke of magic, that the image was projected?

The presence that rose thus so strangely beside the waters, is expressive of what in the ways of a thousand years men

[1] Yet for Vasari there was some further magic of crimson in the lips and cheeks, lost for us.

had come to desire. Hers is the head upon which all 'the ends of the world are come,'* and the eyelids are a little weary. It is a beauty wrought out from within upon the flesh, the deposit, little cell by cell, of strange thoughts and fantastic reveries and exquisite passions. Set it for a moment beside one of those white Greek goddesses or beautiful women of antiquity, and how would they be troubled by this beauty, into which the soul with all its maladies has passed! All the thoughts and experience of the world have etched and moulded there, in that which they have of power to refine and make expressive the outward form, the animalism of Greece, the lust of Rome, the mysticism of the middle age with its spiritual ambition and imaginative loves, the return of the Pagan world, the sins of the Borgias. She is older than the rocks among which she sits; like the vampire, she has been dead many times, and learned the secrets of the grave; and has been a diver in deep seas, and keeps their fallen day about her; and trafficked for strange webs with Eastern merchants: and, as Leda, was the mother of Helen of Troy, and, as Saint Anne, the mother of Mary; and all this has been to her but as the sound of lyres and flutes, and lives only in the delicacy with which it has moulded the changing lineaments, and tinged the eyelids and the hands. The fancy of a perpetual life, sweeping together ten thousand experiences, is an old one; and modern philosophy has conceived the idea of humanity as wrought upon by, and summing up in itself, all modes of thought and life. Certainly Lady Lisa might stand as the embodiment of the old fancy, the symbol of the modern idea.

During these years at Florence Leonardo's history is the history of his art; for himself, he is lost in the bright cloud of it. The outward history begins again in 1502, with a wild journey through central Italy, which he makes as the chief engineer of Cæsar Borgia. The biographer, putting together the stray jottings of his manuscripts, may follow him through every day of it, up the strange tower of Siena, elastic like a bent bow, down to the seashore at Piombino, each place appearing as fitfully as in a fever dream.

One other great work was left for him to do, a work all

trace of which soon vanished, *The Battle of the Standard*, in which he had Michelangelo for his rival. The citizens of Florence, desiring to decorate the walls of the great council-chamber, had offered the work for competition, and any subject might be chosen from the Florentine wars of the fifteenth century. Michelangelo chose for his cartoon an incident of the war with Pisa, in which the Florentine soldiers, bathing in the Arno, are surprised by the sound of trumpets, and run to arms. His design has reached us only in an old engraving, which helps us less perhaps than our remembrance of the background of his *Holy Family* in the *Uffizii* to imagine in what superhuman form, such as might have beguiled the heart of an earlier world, those figures ascended out of the water. Leonardo chose an incident from the battle of Anghiari, in which two parties of soldiers fight for a standard. Like Michelangelo's, his cartoon is lost, and has come to us only in sketches, and in a fragment of Rubens. Through the accounts given we may discern some lust of terrible things in it, so that even the horses tore each other with their teeth. And yet one fragment of it, in a drawing of his at Florence, is far different—a waving field of lovely armour, the chased edgings running like lines of sunlight from side to side. Michelangelo was twenty-seven years old; Leonardo more than fifty; and Raphael, then nineteen years of age, visiting Florence for the first time, came and watched them as they worked.

We catch a glimpse of Leonardo again, at Rome in 1514, surrounded by his mirrors and vials and furnaces, making strange toys that seemed alive of wax and quicksilver. The hesitation which had haunted him all through life, and made him like one under a spell, was upon him now with double force. No one had ever carried political indifferentism further; it had always been his philosophy to 'fly before the storm';* he is for the Sforzas, or against them, as the tide of their fortune turns. Yet now, in the political society of Rome, he came to be suspected of secret French sympathies. It paralysed him to find himself among enemies; and he turned wholly to France, which had long courted him.

France was about to become an Italy more Italian than

Italy itself. Francis the First,* like Lewis the Twelfth before him, was attracted by the *finesse* of Leonardo's work; *La Gioconda* was already in his cabinet, and he offered Leonardo the little *Château de Clou*, with its vineyards and meadows, in the pleasant valley of the Masse, just outside the walls of the town of Amboise, where, especially in the hunting season, the court then frequently resided. *A Monsieur Lyonard, peinteur du Roy pour Amboyse*:—so the letter of Francis the First is headed. It opens a prospect, one of the most interesting in the history of art, where, in a peculiarly blent atmosphere, Italian art dies away as a French exotic.

Two questions remain, after much busy antiquarianism, concerning Leonardo's death—the question of the exact form of his religion, and the question whether Francis the First was present at the time. They are of about equally little importance in the estimate of Leonardo's genius. The directions in his will concerning the thirty masses and the great candles for the church of Saint Florentin are things of course, their real purpose being immediate and practical; and on no theory of religion could these hurried offices be of much consequence. We forget them in speculating how one who had been always so desirous of beauty, but desired it always in such precise and definite forms, as hands or flowers or hair, looked forward now into the vague land, and experienced the last curiosity.

1869.

THE SCHOOL OF GIORGIONE

IT is the mistake of much popular criticism to regard poetry, music, and painting—all the various products of art—as but translations into different languages of one and the same fixed quantity of imaginative thought, supplemented by certain technical qualities of colour, in painting; of sound, in music; of rhythmical words, in poetry. In this way, the sensuous element in art, and with it almost everything in art that is essentially artistic, is made a matter of indifference; and a clear apprehension of the opposite principle—that the sensuous material of each art brings with it a special phase or quality of beauty, untranslatable into the forms of any other, an order of impressions distinct in kind—is the beginning of all true æsthetic criticism. For, as art addresses not pure sense, still less the pure intellect, but the 'imaginative reason'* through the senses, there are differences of kind in æsthetic beauty, corresponding to the differences in kind of the gifts of sense themselves. Each art, therefore, having its own peculiar and untranslatable sensuous charm, has its own special mode of reaching the imagination, its own special responsibilities to its material. One of the functions of æsthetic criticism is to define these limitations; to estimate the degree in which a given work of art fulfils its responsibilities to its special material; to note in a picture that true pictorial charm, which is neither a mere poetical thought or sentiment, on the one hand, nor a mere result of communicable technical skill in colour or design, on the other; to define in a poem that true poetical quality, which is neither descriptive nor meditative merely, but comes of an inventive handling of rhythmical language, the element of song in the singing; to note in music the musical charm, that essential music, which presents no words, no matter of sentiment or thought, separable from the special form in which it is conveyed to us.

To such a philosophy of the variations of the beautiful, Lessing's analysis of the spheres of sculpture and poetry, in the *Laocoon*,* was an important contribution. But a true appreciation of these things is possible only in the light of a whole system of such art-casuistries. Now painting is the art in the criticism of which this truth most needs enforcing, for it is in popular judgments on pictures that the false generalisation of all art into forms of poetry is most prevalent. To suppose that all is mere technical acquirement in delineation or touch, working through and addressing itself to the intelligence, on the one side, or a merely poetical, or what may be called literary interest, addressed also to the pure intelligence, on the other:—this is the way of most spectators, and of many critics, who have never caught sight all the time of that true pictorial quality which lies between, unique pledge, as it is, of the possession of the pictorial gift, that inventive or creative handling of pure line and colour, which, as almost always in Dutch painting, as often also in the works of Titian or Veronese, is quite independent of anything definitely poetical in the subject it accompanies. It is the *drawing*—the design projected from that peculiar pictorial temperament or constitution, in which, while it may possibly be ignorant of true anatomical proportions, all things whatever, all poetry, all ideas however abstract or obscure, float up as visible scene or image: it is the *colouring*— that weaving of light, as of just perceptible gold threads, through the dress, the flesh, the atmosphere, in Titian's *Lace-girl*, that staining of the whole fabric of the thing with a new, delightful physical quality. This *drawing*, then—the arabesque traced in the air by Tintoret's flying figures, by Titian's forest branches; this colouring—the magic conditions of light and hue in the atmosphere of Titian's *Lace-girl*, or Rubens's *Descent from the Cross*:—these essential pictorial qualities must first of all delight the sense, delight it as directly and sensuously as a fragment of Venetian glass; and through this delight alone become the vehicle of whatever poetry or science may lie beyond them in the intention of the composer. In its primary aspect, a great picture has no more definite message for us than an accidental play of sunlight and shadow for a few moments on the wall or floor: is itself, in truth, a space of such fallen light, caught as the colours are in an Eastern carpet, but refined upon, and dealt with more

subtly and exquisitely than by nature itself. And this primary and essential condition fulfilled, we may trace the
coming of poetry into painting, by fine gradations upwards;
from Japanese fan-painting, for instance, where we get,
first, only abstract colour; then, just a little interfused sense
of the poetry of flowers; then, sometimes, perfect flower-
painting; and so, onwards, until in Titian we have, as his
poetry in the *Ariadne*, so actually a touch of true childlike
humour in the diminutive, quaint figure with its silk gown,
which ascends the temple stairs, in his picture of the *Presen-
tation of the Virgin*, at Venice.

But although each art has thus its own specific order of
impressions, and an untranslatable charm, while a just
apprehension of the ultimate differences of the arts is the
beginning of æsthetic criticism; yet it is noticeable that, in its
special mode of handling its given material, each art may be
observed to pass into the condition of some other art, by
what German critics term an *Anders-streben*—a partial aliena-
tion from its own limitations, through which the arts are
able, not indeed to supply the place of each other, but
reciprocally to lend each other new forces.

Thus, some of the most delightful music seems to be
always approaching to figure, to pictorial definition. Architecture, again, though it has its own laws—laws esoteric
enough, as the true architect knows only too well—yet
sometimes aims at fulfilling the conditions of a picture, as in
the *Arena* chapel;* or of sculpture, as in the flawless unity of
Giotto's tower at Florence; and often finds a true poetry, as
in those strangely twisted staircases of the *châteaux* of the
country of the Loire, as if it were intended that among their
odd turnings the actors in a theatrical mode of life might
pass each other unseen; there being a poetry also of memory
and of the mere effect of time, by which architecture often
profits greatly. Thus, again, sculpture aspires out of the hard
limitation of pure form towards colour, or its equivalent;
poetry also, in many ways, finding guidance from the other
arts, the analogy between a Greek tragedy and a work of
Greek sculpture, between a sonnet and a relief, of French
poetry generally with the art of engraving, being more than

mere figures of speech; and all the arts in common aspiring towards the principle of music; music being the typical, or ideally consummate art, the object of the great *Anders-streben* of all art, of all that is artistic, or partakes of artistic qualities.

All art constantly aspires towards the condition of music. For while in all other kinds of art it is possible to distinguish the matter from the form, and the understanding can always make this distinction, yet it is the constant effort of art to obliterate it. That the mere matter of a poem, for instance, its subject, namely, its given incidents or situation—that the mere matter of a picture, the actual circumstances of an event, the actual topography of a landscape—should be nothing without the form, the spirit, of the handling, that this form, this mode of handling, should become an end in itself, should penetrate every part of the matter: this is what all art constantly strives after, and achieves in different degrees.

This abstract language becomes clear enough, if we think of actual examples. In an actual landscape we see a long white road, lost suddenly on the hill-verge. That is the matter of one of the etchings of M. Alphonse Legros:* only, in this etching, it is informed by an indwelling solemnity of expression, seen upon it or half-seen, within the limits of an exceptional moment, or caught from his own mood perhaps, but which he maintains as the very essence of the thing, throughout his work. Sometimes a momentary hint of stormy light may invest a homely or too familiar scene with a character which might well have been drawn from the deep places of the imagination. Then we might say that this particular effect of light, this sudden inweaving of gold thread through the texture of the haystack, and the poplars, and the grass, gives the scene artistic qualities, that it is like a picture. And such tricks of circumstance are commonest in landscape which has little salient character of its own; because, in such scenery, all the material details are so easily absorbed by that informing expression of passing light, and elevated, throughout their whole extent, to a new and delightful effect by it. And hence the superiority, for most conditions of the picturesque, of a river-side in France to a Swiss valley, because, on the French river-side, mere topography, the simple material, counts for so little, and, all being very pure, untouched, and tranquil in itself, mere light and shade have such easy work in modulating it to one dominant tone. The Venetian landscape, on the other hand, has in its material conditions much which is hard, or harshly definite; but the masters of the Venetian school have shown themselves little burdened by them. Of its Alpine background they retain certain abstracted elements only, of cool colour and tranquillising line; and they use its actual details, the brown windy turrets, the straw-coloured fields, the forest arabesques, but as the notes of a music which duly accompanies the presence of their men and women, presenting us with the spirit or essence only of a certain sort of landscape—a country of the pure reason or half-imaginative memory.

Poetry, again, works with words addressed in the first instance to the pure intelligence; and it deals, most often, with a definite subject or situation. Sometimes it may find a noble and quite legitimate function in the conveyance of moral or political aspiration, as often in the poetry of Victor Hugo. In such instances it is easy enough for the understanding to distinguish between the matter and the form, however much the matter, the subject, the element which is addressed to the mere intelligence, has been penetrated by the informing, artistic spirit. But the ideal types of poetry are those in which this distinction is reduced to its *minimum*; so that lyrical poetry, precisely because in it we are least able to detach the matter from the form, without a deduction of something from that matter itself, is, at least artistically, the highest and most complete form of poetry. And the very perfection of such poetry often appears to depend, in part, on a certain suppression or vagueness of mere subject, so that the meaning reaches us through ways not distinctly traceable by the understanding, as in some of the most imaginative compositions of William Blake, and often in Shakespeare's songs, as preeminently in that song of Mariana's page* in *Measure for Measure*, in which the kindling force and poetry of the whole play seems to pass for a moment into an actual strain of music.

And this principle holds good of all things that partake in any degree of artistic qualities, of the furniture of our houses, and of dress, for instance, of life itself, of gesture and speech, and the details of daily intercourse; these also, for the wise, being susceptible of a suavity and charm, caught from the way in which they are done, which gives them a worth in themselves. Herein, again, lies what is valuable and justly attractive, in what is called the fashion of a time, which elevates the trivialities of speech, and manner, and dress, into 'ends in themselves,' and gives them a mysterious grace and attractiveness in the doing of them.

Art, then, is thus always striving to be independent of the mere intelligence, to become a matter of pure perception, to get rid of its responsibilities to its subject or material; the ideal examples of poetry and painting being those in which the constituent elements of the composition are so welded together, that the material or subject no longer strikes the intellect only; nor the form, the eye or the ear only; but form and matter, in their union or identity, present one single effect to the 'imaginative reason,' that complex faculty for which every thought and feeling is twin-born with its sensible analogue or symbol.

It is the art of music which most completely realises this artistic ideal, this perfect identification of matter and form. In its consummate moments, the end is not distinct from the means, the form from the matter, the subject from the expression; they inhere in and completely saturate each other; and to it, therefore, to the condition of its perfect moments, all the arts may be supposed constantly to tend and aspire. In music, then, rather than in poetry, is to be found the true type or measure of perfected art. Therefore, although each art has its incommunicable element, its untranslatable order of impressions, its unique mode of reaching the 'imaginative reason,' yet the arts may be represented as continually struggling after the law or principle of music, to a condition which music alone completely realises; and one of the chief functions of æsthetic criticism, dealing with the products of art, new or old, is to estimate the degree in which each of those products approaches, in this sense, to musical law.

By no school of painters have the necessary limitations of the art of painting been so unerringly though instinctively apprehended, and the essence of what is pictorial in a picture so justly conceived, as by the school of Venice; and the train of thought suggested in what has been now said is, perhaps, a not unfitting introduction to a few pages about Giorgione, who, though much has been taken by recent criticism from what was reputed to be his work, yet, more entirely than any other painter, sums up, in what we know of himself and his art, the spirit of the Venetian school.

The beginnings of Venetian painting link themselves to the last, stiff, half-barbaric splendours of Byzantine decoration, and are but the introduction into the crust of marble and gold on the walls of the *Duomo* of Murano, or of *Saint Mark's*, of a little more of human expression. And throughout the course of its later development, always subordinate to architectural effect, the work of the Venetian school never escaped from the influence of its beginnings. Unassisted, and therefore unperplexed, by naturalism, religious mysticism, philosophical theories, it had no Giotto, no Angelico, no Botticelli. Exempt from the stress of thought and sentiment, which taxed so severely the resources of the generations of Florentine artists, those earlier Venetian painters, down to Carpaccio and the Bellini, seem never for a moment to have been so much as tempted to lose sight of the scope of their art in its strictness, or to forget that painting must be before all things decorative, a thing for the eye, a space of colour on the wall, only more dexterously blent than the marking of its precious stone or the chance interchange of sun and shade upon it:—this, to begin and end with; whatever higher matter of thought, or poetry, or religious reverie might play its part therein, between. At last, with final mastery of all the technical secrets of his art, and with somewhat more than 'a spark of the divine fire' to his share, comes Giorgione. He is the inventor of *genre*, of those easily movable pictures which serve neither for uses of devotion, nor of allegorical or historic teaching—little groups of real men and women, amid congruous furniture or landscape—morsels of actual life, conversation or music or play, but refined upon or idealised, till they come to seem like glimpses of life from afar. Those spaces of more cunningly blent colour, obediently filling their places, hitherto, in a mere architectural scheme, Giorgione detaches from the wall. He frames them by the hands of some skilful carver, so that people may move them readily and take with them where they go, as one might a poem in manuscript, or a musical instrument, to be used, at will, as a means of self-education, stimulus or solace, coming like an animated presence, into one's cabinet, to enrich the air as with some choice aroma, and, like persons, live with us, for a day or a lifetime. Of all art such as this, art which has played so large a part in men's culture since that time, Giorgione is the initiator. Yet in him too that old Venetian clearness or justice, in the apprehension of the essential limitations of the pictorial art, is still undisturbed. While he interfuses his painted work with a high-strung sort of poetry, caught directly from a singularly rich and high-strung sort of life, yet in his selection of subject, or phase of subject, in the subordination of mere subject to pictorial design, to the main purpose of a picture, he is typical of that aspiration of all the arts towards music, which I have endeavoured to explain,— towards the perfect identification of matter and form.

Born so near to Titian, though a little before him, that these two companion pupils of the aged Giovanni Bellini* may almost be called contemporaries, Giorgione stands to Titian in something like the relationship of Sordello to Dante, in Browning's poem.* Titian, when he leaves Bellini, becomes, in turn, the pupil of Giorgione. He lives in constant labour more than sixty years after Giorgione is in his grave; and with such fruit, that hardly one of the greater towns of Europe is without some fragment of his work. But the slightly older man, with his so limited actual product (what remains to us of it seeming, when narrowly explained, to reduce itself to almost one picture, like Sordello's one fragment of lovely verse) yet expresses, in elementary motive and principle, that spirit—itself the final acquisition of all the long endeavours of Venetian art—which Titian spreads over his whole life's activity.

And, as we might expect, something fabulous and illusive has always mingled itself in the brilliancy of Giorgione's fame. The exact relationship to him of many works—drawings, portraits, painted idylls—often fascinating enough, which in various collections went by his name, was from the first uncertain. Still, six or eight famous pictures at Dresden, Florence and the Louvre, were with no doubt attributed to him, and in these, if anywhere, something of the splendour of the old Venetian humanity seemed to have been preserved. But of those six or eight famous pictures it is now known that only one is certainly from Giorgione's hand. The accomplished science of the subject has come at last, and, as in other instances, has not made the past more real for us, but assured us only that we possess less of it than we seemed to possess. Much of the work on which Giorgione's immediate fame depended, work done for instantaneous effect, in all probability passed away almost within his own age, like the frescoes on the façade of the *fondaco dei Tedeschi* at Venice, some crimson traces of which, however, still give a strange additional touch of splendour to the scene of the *Rialto*. And then there is a barrier or borderland, a period about the middle of the sixteenth century, in passing through which the tradition miscarries, and the true outlines of Giorgione's work and person are obscured. It became fashionable for wealthy lovers of art, with no criticial standard of authenticity, to collect so-called works of Giorgione, and a multitude of imitations came into circulation. And now, in the 'new Vasari[1],' the great traditional reputation, woven with so profuse demand on men's admiration, has been scrutinised thread by thread; and what remains of the most vivid and stimulating of Venetian masters, a live flame, as it seemed, in those old shadowy times, has been reduced almost to a name by his most recent critics.

Yet enough remains to explain why the legend grew up above the name, why the name attached itself, in many

[1] Crowe and Cavalcaselle: *History of Painting in North Italy.*

instances, to the bravest work of other men. The *Concert* in the *Pitti* Palace, in which a monk, with cowl and tonsure, touches the keys of a harpsichord, while a clerk, placed behind him, grasps the handle of a viol, and a third, with cap and plume, seems to wait upon the true interval for beginning to sing, is undoubtedly Giorgione's. The outline of the lifted finger, the trace of the plume, the very threads of the fine linen, which fasten themselves on the memory, in the moment before they are lost altogether in that calm unearthly glow, the skill which has caught the waves of wandering sound, and fixed them for ever on the lips and hands—these are indeed the master's own; and the criticism which, while dismissing so much hitherto believed to be Giorgione's, has established the claims of this one picture, has left it among the most precious things in the world of art.

It is noticeable that the 'distinction' of this *Concert*, its sustained evenness of perfection, alike in design, in execution, and in choice of personal type, becomes for the 'new Vasari' the standard of Giorgione's genuine work. Finding here sufficient to explain his influence, and the true seal of mastery, its authors assign to Pellegrino da San Daniele the *Holy Family* in the Louvre, in consideration of certain points where it comes short of this standard. Such shortcoming however will hardly diminish the spectator's enjoyment of a singular charm of liquid air, with which the whole picture seems instinct, filling the eyes and lips, the very garments, of its sacred personages, with some wind-searched brightness and energy; of which fine air the blue peak, clearly defined in the distance, is, as it were, the visible pledge. Similarly, another favourite picture in the Louvre, subject of a delightful sonnet by a poet[1] whose own painted work often comes to mind as one ponders over these precious things—the *Fête Champêtre*, is assigned to an imitator of Sebastian del Piombo; and the *Tempest*, in the Academy at Venice, to Paris Bordone, or perhaps to 'some advanced craftsman of the sixteenth century.' From the gallery at Dresden, the *Knight embracing a Lady*, where the knight's broken gauntlet seems to

---

[1] Dante Gabriel Rossetti.

mark some well-known pause in a story we would willingly hear the rest of, is conceded to 'a Brescian hand,' and *Jacob meeting Rachel* to a pupil of Palma. And then, whatever their charm, we are called on to give up the *Ordeal*, and the *Finding of Moses* with its jewel-like pools of water, perhaps to Bellini.

Nor has the criticism, which thus so freely diminishes the number of his authentic works, added anything important to the well-known outline of the life and personality of the man: only, it has fixed one or two dates, one or two circumstances, a little more exactly. Giorgione was born before the year 1477, and spent his childhood at Castelfranco, where the last crags of the Venetian Alps break down romantically, with something of park-like grace, to the plain. A natural child of the family of the Barbarelli by a peasant-girl of Vedelago, he finds his way early into the circle of notable persons—people of courtesy. He is initiated into those differences of personal type, manner, and even of dress, which are best understood there—that 'distinction' of the *Concert** of the *Pitti* Palace. Not far from his home lives Catherine of Cornara, formerly Queen of Cyprus;* and, up in the towers which still remain, Tuzio Costanzo,* the famous *condottiére*, a picturesque remnant of medieval manners, amid a civilisation rapidly changing. Giorgione paints their portraits; and when Tuzio's son, Matteo, dies in early youth, adorns in his memory a chapel in the church of Castelfranco, painting on this occasion, perhaps, the altar-piece, foremost among his authentic works, still to be seen there, with the figure of the warrior-saint, Liberale, of which the original little study in oil, with the delicately gleaming, silver-grey armour, is one of the greater treasures of the National Gallery. In that figure, as in some other knightly personages attributed to him, people have supposed the likeness of the painter's own presumably gracious presence. Thither, at last, he is himself brought home from Venice, early dead, but celebrated. It happened, about his thirty-fourth year, that in one of those parties at which he entertained his friends with music, he met a certain lady of whom he became greatly enamoured, and 'they rejoiced greatly,' says Vasari,* 'the one and the other, in their loves.'

And two quite different legends concerning it agree in this, that it was through this lady he came by his death; Ridolfi* relating that, being robbed of her by one of his pupils, he died of grief at the double treason; Vasari, that she being secretly stricken of the plague, and he making his visits to her as usual, Giorgione took the sickness from her mortally, along with her kisses, and so briefly departed.

But, although the number of Giorgione's extant works has been thus limited by recent criticism, all is not done when the real and the traditional elements in what concerns him have been discriminated; for, in what is connected with a great name, much that is not real is often very stimulating. For the æsthetic philosopher, therefore, over and above the real Giorgione and his authentic extant works, there remains the *Giorgionesque* also—an influence, a spirit or type in art, active in men so different as those to whom many of his supposed works are really assignable. A veritable school, in fact, grew together out of all those fascinating works rightly or wrongly attributed to him; out of many copies from, or variations on him, by unknown or uncertain workmen, whose drawings and designs were, for various reasons, prized as his; out of the immediate impression he made upon his contemporaries, and with which he continued in men's minds; out of many traditions of subject and treatment, which really descend from him to our own time, and by retracing which we fill out the original image. Giorgione thus becomes a sort of impersonation of Venice itself, its projected reflex or ideal, all that was intense or desirable in it crystallising about the memory of this wonderful young man.

And now, finally, let me illustrate some of the characteristics of this *School of Giorgione*, as we may call it, which, for most of us, notwithstanding all that negative criticism of the 'new Vasari,' will still identify itself with those famous pictures at Florence, at Dresden and Paris. A certain artistic ideal is there defined for us—the conception of a peculiar aim and procedure in art, which we may understand as the *Giorgionesque*, wherever we find it, whether in Venetian work generally, or in work of our own time. Of this the *Concert*, that undoubted work of Giorgione in the *Pitti* Palace, is the typical instance, and a pledge authenticating the connexion of the school, and the spirit of the school, with the master.

I have spoken of a certain interpretation of the matter or subject of a work of art with the form of it, a condition realised absolutely only in music, as the condition to which every form of art is perpetually aspiring. In the art of painting, the attainment of this ideal condition, this perfect interpenetration of the subject with the elements of colour and design, depends, of course, in great measure, on dexterous choice of that subject, or phase of subject; and such choice is one of the secrets of Giorgione's school. It is the school of *genre*, and employs itself mainly with 'painted idylls,' but, in the production of this pictorial poetry, exercises a wonderful tact in the selecting of such matter as lends itself most readily and entirely to pictorial form, to complete expression by drawing and colour. For although its productions are painted poems, they belong to a sort of poetry which tells itself without an articulated story. The master is pre-eminent for the resolution, the ease and quickness, with which he reproduces instantaneous motion—the lacing-on of armour, with the head bent back so stately—the fainting lady—the embrace, rapid as the kiss, caught with death itself from dying lips—some momentary conjunction of mirrors and polished armour and still water, by which all the sides of a solid image are exhibited at once, solving that casuistical question whether painting can present an object as completely as sculpture. The sudden act, the rapid transition of thought, the passing expression—these he arrests with that vivacity which Vasari has attributed to him, *il fuoco Giorgionesco,** as he terms it. Now it is part of the ideality of the highest sort of dramatic poetry, that it presents us with a kind of profoundly significant and animated instants, a mere gesture, a look, a smile, perhaps—some brief and wholly concrete moment—into which, however, all the motives, all the interests and effects of a long history, have condensed themselves, and which seem to absorb past and future in an intense consciousness of the present. Such ideal instants the school of Giorgione selects, with its admirable tact, from that feverish, tumultuously coloured world of the old citizens of Venice—exquisite pauses in time, in which, arrested thus, we seem to be spectators of all the fulness of existence, and which are like some consummate extract or quintessence of life.

It is to the law or condition of music, as I said, that all art like this is really aspiring; and, in the school of Giorgione, the perfect moments of music itself, the making or hearing of music, song or its accompaniment, are themselves prominent as subjects. On that background of the silence of Venice, so impressive to the modern visitor, the world of Italian music was then forming. In choice of subject, as in all besides, the *Concert* of the *Pitti* Palace is typical of everything that Giorgione, himself an admirable musician, touched with his influence. In sketch or finished picture, in various collections, we may follow it through many intricate variations—men fainting at music; music at the pool-side while people fish, or mingled with the sound of the pitcher in the well, or heard across running water, or among the flocks; the tuning of instruments; people with intent faces, as if listening, like those described by Plato in an ingenious passage of the Republic,* to detect the smallest interval of musical sound, the smallest undulation in the air, or feeling for music in thought on a stringless instrument, ear and finger refining themselves infinitely, in the appetite for sweet sound; a momentary touch of an instrument in the twilight, as one passes through some unfamiliar room, in a chance company.

In these then, the favourite incidents of Giorgione's school, music or the musical intervals in our existence, life itself is conceived as a sort of listening—listening to music, to the reading of Bandello's novels,* to the sound of water, to time as it flies. Often such moments are really our moments of play, and we are surprised at the unexpected blessedness of what may seem our least important part of time; not merely because play is in many instances that to which people really apply their own best powers, but also because at such times, the stress of our servile, everyday attentiveness being relaxed, the happier powers in things without are permitted free passage, and have their way with us. And so, from music, the school of Giorgione passes often to the play which is like music; to those masques in which men avowedly do but play at real life, like children 'dressing-up,' disguised in the strange old Italian dresses, particoloured, or fantastic with embroidery and furs, of which the master was so curious a designer, and which, above all the spotless white linen at wrist and throat, he painted so dexterously.

But when people are happy in this thirsty land water will not be far off; and in the school of Giorgione, the presence of water—the well, or marble-rimmed pool, the drawing or pouring of water, as the woman pours it from a pitcher with her jewelled hand in the *Fête Champêtre*,* listening, perhaps, to the cool sound as it falls, blent with the music of the pipes—is as characteristic, and almost as suggestive, as that of music itself. And the landscape feels, and is glad of it also—a landscape full of clearness, of the effects of water, of fresh rain newly passed through the air, and collected into the grassy channels. The air, moreover, in the school of Giorgione, seems as vivid as the people who breathe it, and literally empyrean, all impurities being burnt out of it, and no taint, no floating particle of anything but its own proper elements allowed to subsist within it.

Its scenery is such as in England we call 'park scenery,' with some elusive refinement felt about the rustic buildings, the choice grass, the grouped trees, the undulations deftly economised for graceful effect. Only, in Italy all natural things are as it were woven through and through with gold thread, even the cypress revealing it among the folds of its blackness. And it is with gold dust, or gold thread, that these Venetian painters seem to work, spinning its fine filaments, through the solemn human flesh, away into the white plastered walls of the thatched huts. The harsher details of the mountains recede to a harmonious distance, the one peak of rich blue above the horizon remaining but as the sensible warrant of that due coolness which is all we need ask here of the Alps, with their dark rains and streams. Yet what real, airy space, as the eye passes from level to level, through the long-drawn valley in which Jacob embraces Rachel among the flocks!* Nowhere is there a truer instance of that balance, that modulated unison of landscape and persons—of the human image and its accessories—already noticed as characteristic of the Venetian school, so that, in it, neither personage nor scenery is ever a mere pretext for the other.

Something like this seems to me to be the *vraie vérité** about Giorgione, if I may adopt a serviceable expression, by which the French recognise those more liberal and durable impressions which, in respect of any really considerable person or subject, anything that has at all intricately occupied men's attention, lie beyond, and must supplement, the narrower range of the strictly ascertained facts about it. In this, Giorgione is but an illustration of a valuable general caution we may abide by in all criticism. As regards Giorgione himself, we have indeed to take note of all those negations and exceptions, by which, at first sight, a 'new Vasari' seems merely to have confused our apprehension of a delightful object, to have explained away in our inheritance from past time what seemed of high value there. Yet it is not with a full understanding even of those exceptions that one can leave off just at this point. Properly qualified, such exceptions are but a salt of genuineness in our knowledge; and beyond all those strictly ascertained facts, we must take note of that indirect influence by which one like Giorgione, for instance, enlarges his permanent efficacy and really makes himself felt in our culture. In a just impression of that, is the essential truth, the *vraie vérité*, concerning him.

1877.

JOACHIM DU BELLAY

In the middle of the sixteenth century, when the spirit of the Renaissance was everywhere, and people had begun to look back with distaste on the works of the middle age, the old Gothic manner had still one chance more, in borrowing something from the rival which was about to supplant it. In this way there was produced, chiefly in France, a new and peculiar phase of taste with qualities and a charm of its own, blending the somewhat attenuated grace of Italian ornament with the general outlines of northern design. It created the *Château de Gaillon*, as you may still see it in the delicate engravings of Isräel Silvestre*—a Gothic donjon veiled faintly by a surface of dainty Italian traceries—Chenonceaux, Blois, Chambord, and the church of Brou. In painting, there came from Italy workmen like *Maître Roux** and the masters of the school of Fontainebleau, to have their later Italian voluptuousness attempered by the naïve and silvery qualities of the native style; and it was characteristic of these painters that they were most successful in painting on glass, an art so essentially medieval. Taking it up where the middle age had left it, they found their whole work among the last subtleties of colour and line; and keeping within the true limits of their material, they got quite a new order of effects from it, and felt their way to refinements on colour never dreamed of by those older workmen, the glass-painters of Chartres or Le Mans. What is called the *Renaissance in France* is thus not so much the introduction of a wholly new taste ready-made from Italy, but rather the finest and subtlest phase of the middle age itself, its last fleeting splendour and temperate Saint Martin's summer. In poetry, the Gothic spirit in France had produced a thousand songs; so in the Renaissance, French poetry too did but borrow something to blend with a native growth, and the poems of Ronsard,* with their ingenuity, their delicately figured surfaces, their slightness, their fanciful combinations of rhyme, are the correlative of the traceries of the house of Jacques Cœur at Bourges, or the *Maison de Justice* at Rouen.

There was indeed something in the native French taste naturally akin to that Italian *finesse*. The characteristic of French work had always been a certain nicety, a remarkable daintiness of hand, *une netteté remarquable d'exécution*. In the paintings of François Clouet, for example, or rather of the Clouets*—for there was a whole family of them—painters remarkable for their resistance to Italian influences, there is a silveriness of colour and a clearness of expression which distinguish them very definitely from their Flemish neighbours, Hemling* or the Van Eycks.* And this nicety is not less characteristic of old French poetry. A light, aerial delicacy, a simple elegance—*une netteté remarquable d'exécution*: these are essential characteristics alike of Villon's* poetry, and of the *Hours of Anne of Brittany*.* They are characteristic too of a hundred French Gothic carvings and traceries. Alike in the old Gothic cathedrals, and in their counterpart, the old Gothic *chansons de geste*,* the rough and ponderous mass becomes, as if by passing for a moment into happier conditions, or through a more gracious stratum of air, graceful and refined, like the carved ferneries on the granite church at Folgoat, or the lines which describe the fair priestly hands of Archbishop Turpin, in the song of Roland;* although below both alike there is a fund of mere Gothic strength, or heaviness.[1]

Now Villon's songs and Clouet's painting are like these. It is the higher touch making itself felt here and there, betraying itself, like nobler blood in a lower stock, by a fine line or gesture or expression, the turn of a wrist, the tapering of a finger. In Ronsard's time that rougher element seemed likely to predominate. No one can turn over the pages of Rabelais* without feeling how much need there was of softening, of castigation. To effect this softening is the object of the revolution in poetry which is connected with Ronsard's name. Casting about for the means of thus refining upon and

---

[1] The purely artistic aspects of this subject have been interpreted, in a work of great taste and learning, by Mrs. Mark Pattison.— *The Renaissance of Art in France*.

saving the character of French literature, he accepted that
influx of Renaissance taste, which, leaving the buildings, the
language, the art, the poetry of France, at bottom, what they
were, old French Gothic still, gilds their surfaces with a
strange, delightful, foreign aspect passing over all that
northern land, in itself neither deeper nor more permanent
than a chance effect of light. He reinforces, he doubles the
French daintiness by Italian *finesse*. Thereupon, nearly all
the force and all the seriousness of French work disappear;
only the elegance, the aerial touch, the perfect manner
remain. But this elegance, this manner, this daintiness of
execution are consummate, and have an unmistakable
æsthetic value.

So the old French *chanson*, which, like the old northern
Gothic ornament, though it sometimes refined itself into a
sort of weird elegance, was often, in its essence, something
rude and formless, became in the hands of Ronsard a
Pindaric ode.* He gave it structure, a sustained system,
strophe and *antistrophe*, and taught it a changefulness and
variety of metre which keep the curiosity always excited, so
that the very aspect of it, as it lies written on the page,
carried the eye lightly onwards, and of which this is a good
instance:—

> Avril, la grace, et le ris
> > De Cypris,
> Le flair et la douce haleine;
> Avril, le parfum des dieux,
> > Qui, des cieux,
> Sentent l'odeur de la plaine;
>
> C'est toy, courtois et gentil,
> > Qui, d'exil
> Retire ces passageres,
> Ces arondelles qui vont,
> > Et qui sont
> Du printemps les messageres.*

That is not by Ronsard, but by Remy Belleau, for Ronsard
soon came to have a school. Six other poets threw in their lot

with him in his literary revolution,—this Remy Belleau, Antoine de Baïf, Pontus de Tyard, Étienne Jodelle, Jean Daurat, and lastly Joachim du Bellay; and with that strange love of emblems which is characteristic of the time, which covered all the works of Francis the First with the salamander, and all the works of Henry the Second with the double crescent, and all the works of Anne of Brittany with the knotted cord, they called themselves the *Pleiad*,* seven in all, although, as happens with the celestial Pleiad, if you scrutinise this constellation of poets more carefully you may find there a great number of minor stars.

The first note of this literary revolution was struck by Joachim du Bellay in a little tract written at the early age of twenty-four, which coming to us through three centuries seems of yesterday, so full is it of those delicate critical distinctions which are sometimes supposed peculiar to modern writers. The piece has for its title *La Deffense et Illustration de la langue Françoyse*; and its problem is how to illustrate or ennoble the French language, to give it lustre. We are accustomed to speak of the varied critical and creative movement of the fifteenth and sixteenth centuries as the *Renaissance*, and because we have a single name for it we may sometimes fancy that there was more unity in the thing itself than there really was. Even the Reformation, that other great movement of the fifteenth and sixteenth centuries, had far less unity, far less of combined action, than is at first sight supposed; and the Renaissance was infinitely less united, less conscious of combined action, than the Reformation. But if anywhere the Renaissance became conscious, as a German philosopher might say, if ever it was understood as a systematic movement by those who took part in it, it is in this little book of Joachim du Bellay's, which it is impossible to read without feeling the excitement, the animation, of change, of discovery. 'It is a remarkable fact,' says M. Sainte-Beuve, 'and an inversion of what is true of other languages, that, in French, prose has always had the precedence over poetry.'* Du Bellay's prose is perfectly transparent, flexible, and chaste. In many ways it is a more characteristic example of the culture of the *Pleiad* than any

of its verse; and those who love the whole movement of
which the *Pleiad* is a part, for a weird foreign grace in it,
and may be looking about for a true specimen of it, cannot
have a better than Joachim du Bellay and this little treatise
of his.

Du Bellay's object is to adjust the existing French culture
to the rediscovered classical culture; and in discussing this
problem, and developing the theories of the *Pleiad*, he has
lighted upon many principles of permanent truth and appli-
cability. There were some who despaired of the French
language altogether, who thought it naturally incapable of
the fulness and elegance of Greek and Latin—*cette élégance et
copie qui est en la langue Greque et Romaine*—that science could
be adequately discussed, and poetry nobly written, only in
the dead languages. 'Those who speak thus,' says Du Bellay,
'make me think of the relics which one may only see through
a little pane of glass, and must not touch with one's hands.
That is what these people do with all branches of culture,
which they keep shut up in Greek and Latin books, not
permitting one to see them otherwise, or transport them out
of dead words into those which are alive, and wing their way
daily through the mouths of men.' 'Languages,' he says
again, 'are not born like plants and trees, some naturally
feeble and sickly, others healthy and strong and apter to bear
the weight of men's conceptions, but all their virtue is
generated in the world of choice and men's freewill concerning them. Therefore, I cannot blame too strongly the
rashness of some of our countrymen, who being anything
rather than Greeks or Latins, depreciate and reject with
more than stoical disdain everything written in French; nor
can I express my surprise at the odd opinion of some learned
men who think that our vulgar tongue is wholly incapable of
erudition and good literature.'

It was an age of translations. Du Bellay himself translated
two books of the *Æneid*, and other poetry, old and new, and
there were some who thought that the translation of the
classical literature was the true means of *ennobling* the French
language:—strangers are ever favourites with us—*nous favori-
sons toujours les étrangers*. Du Bellay moderates their

expectations. 'I do not believe that one can learn the right use of them'—he is speaking of figures and ornament in language—'from translations, because it is impossible to reproduce them with the same grace with which the original author used them. For each language has I know not what peculiarity of its own; and if you force yourself to express the naturalness (*le naïf*) of this in another language, observing the law of translation,—not to expatiate beyond the limits of the author himself, your words will be constrained, cold and ungraceful.' Then he fixes the test of all good translation:—'To prove this, read me Demosthenes and Homer in Latin, Cicero and Virgil in French, and see whether they produce in you the same affections which you experience in reading those authors in the original.'

In this effort to ennoble the French language, to give it grace, number, perfection, and as painters do to their pictures, that last, so desirable, touch—*cette dernière main que nous désirons*—what Du Bellay is really pleading for is his mother-tongue, the language, that is, in which one will have the utmost degree of what is moving and passionate. He recognised of what force the music and dignity of languages are, how they enter into the inmost part of things; and in pleading for the cultivation of the French language, he is pleading for no merely scholastic interest, but for freedom, impulse, reality, not in literature only, but in daily communion of speech. After all, it was impossible to have this impulse in Greek and Latin, dead languages shut up in books as in reliquaries—*péris et mises en reliquaires de livres*. By aid of this starveling stock—*pauvre plante et vergette*—of the French language, he must speak delicately, movingly, if he is ever to speak so at all: that, or none, must be for him the medium of what he calls, in one of his great phrases, *le discours fatal des choses mondaines*—that discourse about affairs which decide men's fates. And it is his patriotism not to despair of it; he sees it already perfect in all elegance and beauty of words— *parfait en toute élégance et vénusté de paroles*.

Du Bellay was born in the disastrous year 1525, the year of the battle of Pavia, and the captivity of Francis the First. His parents died early, and to him, as the younger son, his mother's little estate, *ce petit Liré*, the beloved place of his birth, descended. He was brought up by a brother only a little older than himself; and left to themselves, the two boys passed their lives in day-dreams of military glory. Their education was neglected; 'The time of my youth,' says Du Bellay, 'was lost, like the flower which no shower waters, and no hand cultivates.' He was just twenty years old when the elder brother died, leaving Joachim to be the guardian of his child. It was with regret, with a shrinking sense of incapacity, that he took upon him the burden of this responsibility. Hitherto he had looked forward to the profession of a soldier, hereditary in his family. But at this time a sickness attacked him which brought him cruel sufferings, and seemed likely to be mortal. It was then for the first time that he read the Greek and Latin poets. These studies came too late to make him what he so much desired to be, a trifler in Greek and Latin verse, like so many others of his time now forgotten; instead, they made him a lover of his own homely native tongue, that poor starveling stock of the French language. It was through this fortunate shortcoming in his education that he became national and modern; and he learned afterwards to look back on that wild garden of his youth with only a half-regret. A certain Cardinal du Bellay was the successful member of the family, a man often employed in high official business. To him the thoughts of Joachim turned when it became necessary to choose a profession, and in 1552 he accompanied the Cardinal to Rome. He remained there nearly five years, burdened with the weight of affairs, and languishing with home-sickness. Yet it was under these circumstances that his genius yielded its best fruits. From Rome, so full of pleasurable sensation for men of an imaginative temperament such as his, with all the curiosities of the Renaissance still fresh in it, his thoughts went back painfully, longingly, to the country of the Loire, with its wide expanse of waving corn, its homely pointed roofs of grey slate, and its far-off scent of the sea. He reached home at last, but only to die there, quite suddenly, one wintry day, at the early age of thirty-five.

Much of Du Bellay's poetry illustrates rather the age and school to which he belonged than his own temper and genius. As with the writings of Ronsard and the other poets of the *Pleiad*, its interest depends not so much on the impress of individual genius upon it, as on the circumstance that it was once poetry *à la mode*, that it is part of the manner of a time— a time which made much of manner, and carried it to a high degree of perfection. It is one of the decorations of an age which threw a large part of its energy into the work of decoration. We feel a pensive pleasure in gazing on these faded adornments, and observing how a group of actual men and women pleased themselves long ago. Ronsard's poems are a kind of epitome of his age. Of one side of that age, it is true, of the strenuous, the progressive, the serious movement, which was then going on, there is little; but of the catholic side, the losing side, the forlorn hope, hardly a figure is absent. The Queen of Scots, at whose desire Ronsard published his Odes, reading him in her northern prison, felt that he was bringing back to her the true flavour of her early days in the court of Catherine at the Louvre, with its exotic Italian gaieties.* Those who disliked that poetry, disliked it because they found that age itself distasteful. The poetry of Malherbe* came, with its sustained style and weighty sentiment, but with nothing that set people singing; and the lovers of such poetry saw in the poetry of the *Pleiad* only the latest trumpery of the middle age. But the time arrived when the school of Malherbe also had had its day; and the *Romanticists*,* who in their eagerness for excitement, for strange music and imagery, went back to the works of the middle age, accepted the *Pleiad* too with the rest; and in that new middle age which their genius has evoked, the poetry of the *Pleiad* has found its place. At first, with Malherbe, you may think it, like the architecture, the whole mode of life, the very dresses of that time, fantastic, faded, *rococo*. But if you look long enough to understand it, to conceive its sentiment, you will find that those wanton lines have a spirit guiding their caprices. For there is *style* there; one temper has shaped the whole; and everything that has style, that has been done as no other man or age could have done it, as it could never, for all our trying, be done again, has its true value and interest. Let us dwell upon it for a moment, and try to gather from it that special flower, *ce fleur particulier*, which Ronsard himself tells us every garden has.

It is poetry not for the people, but for a confined circle, for courtiers, great lords and erudite persons, people who desire to be humoured, to gratify a certain refined voluptuousness they have in them. Ronsard loves, or dreams that he loves, a rare and peculiar type of beauty, *la petite pucelle Angevine*, with golden hair and dark eyes. But he has the ambition not only of being a courtier and a lover, but a great scholar also; he is anxious about orthography, about the letter *è Grecque*, the true spelling of Latin names in French writing, and the restoration of the letter *i* to its primitive liberty—*del' i voyelle en sa première liberté*. His poetry is full of quaint, remote learning. He is just a little pedantic, true always to his own express judgment, that to be natural is not enough for one who in poetry desires to produce work worthy of immortality. And therewithal a certain number of Greek words, which charmed Ronsard and his circle by their gaiety and daintiness, and a certain air of foreign elegance about them, crept into the French language; as there were other strange words which the poets of the *Pleiad* forged for themselves, and which had only an ephemeral existence.

With this was united the desire to taste a more exquisite and various music than that of the older French verse, or of the classical poets. The music of the measured, scanned verse of Latin and Greek poetry is one thing; the music of the rhymed, unscanned verse of Villon and the old French poets, *la poésie chantée*, is another. To combine these two kinds of music in a new school of French poetry, to make verse which should scan and rhyme as well, to search out and harmonise the measure of every syllable, and unite it to the swift, flitting, swallow-like motion of rhyme, to penetrate their poetry with a double music—this was the ambition of the *Pleiad*. They are insatiable of music, they cannot have enough of it; they desire a music of greater compass perhaps than words can possibly yield, to drain out the last drops of sweetness which a certain note or accent contains.

It was Goudimel,* the serious and protestant Goudimel, who set Ronsard's songs to music; but except in this eagerness for music the poets of the *Pleiad* seem never quite in earnest. The old Greek and Roman mythology, which the great Italians had found a motive so weighty and severe, becomes with them a mere toy. That 'Lord of terrible aspect,'* *Amor*, has become Love the boy, or the babe. They are full of fine railleries; they delight in diminutives, *ondelette*, *fontelette*, *doucelette*, *Cassandrette*. Their loves are only half real, a vain effort to prolong the imaginative loves of the middle age beyond their natural lifetime. They write love-poems for hire. Like that party of people who tell the tales in Boccaccio's *Decameron*, they form a circle which in an age of great troubles, losses, anxieties, can amuse itself with art, poetry, intrigue. But they amuse themselves with wonderful elegance. And sometimes their gaiety becomes satiric, for, as they play, real passions insinuate themselves, and at least the reality of death. Their dejection at the thought of leaving this fair abode of our common daylight—*le beau sejour du commun jour*—is expressed by them with almost wearisome reiteration. But with this sentiment too they are able to trifle. The imagery of death serves for delicate ornament, and they weave into the airy nothingness of their verses their trite reflexions on the vanity of life. Just so the grotesque details of the charnel-house nest themselves, together with birds and flowers and the fancies of the pagan mythology, in the traceries of the architecture of that time, which wantons in its graceful arabesques with the images of old age and death.

Ronsard became deaf at sixteen; and it was this circumstance which finally determined him to be a man of letters instead of a diplomatist, significantly, one might fancy, of a certain premature agedness, and of the tranquil, temperate sweetness appropriate to that, in the school of poetry which he founded. Its charm is that of a thing not vigorous or original, but full of the grace which comes of long study and reiterated refinements, and many steps repeated, and many angles worn down, with an exquisite faintness, *une fadeur exquise*, a certain tenuity and caducity, as for those who can bear nothing vehement or strong; for princes weary of love, like Francis the First, or of pleasure, like Henry the Third, or of action, like Henry the Fourth.* Its merits are those of the old,—grace and finish, perfect in minute detail. For these people are a little jaded, and have a constant desire for a subdued and delicate excitement, to warm their creeping fancy a little. They love a constant change of rhyme in poetry, and in their houses that strange, fantastic interweaving of thin, reed-like lines, which are a kind of rhetoric in architecture.

But the poetry of the *Pleiad* is true not only to the physiognomy of its age, but also to its country, *ce pays du Vendomois*, the names and scenery of which so often recur in it:—the great Loire, with its long spaces of white sand; the little river Loir; the heathy, upland country, with its scattered pools of water and waste roadsides, and retired manors, with their crazy old feudal defences half fallen into decay; *La Beauce*, where the vast rolling fields seem to anticipate the great western sea itself. It is full of the traits of that country. We see Du Bellay and Ronsard gardening, or hunting with their dogs, or watch the pastimes of a rainy day; and with all this is connected a domesticity, a homeliness and simple goodness, by which the northern country gains upon the south. They have the love of the aged for warmth, and understand the poetry of winter; for they are not far from the Atlantic, and the west wind which comes up from it, turning the poplars white, spares not this new Italy in France. So the fireside often appears, with the pleasures of the frosty season, about the vast emblazoned chimneys of the time, and with a *bonhomie* as of little children, or old people.

It is in Du Bellay's *Olive*, a collection of sonnets in praise of a half-imaginary lady, *Sonnetz a la louange d'Olive*, that these characteristics are most abundant. Here is a perfectly crystallised example:—

D'amour, de grace, et de haulte valeur
   Les feux divins estoient ceinctz et les cieulx
   S'estoient vestuz d'un manteau precieux
   A raiz ardens de diverse couleur:
Tout estoit plein de beauté, de bonheur,
   La mer tranquille, et le vent gracieulx,
   Quand celle la nasquit en ces bas lieux
   Qui a pillé du monde tout l'honneur.
Ell' prist son teint des beux lyz blanchissans,
   Son chef de l'or, ses deux levres des rozes,
   Et du soleil ses yeux resplandissans:
Le ciel usant de liberalité,
   Mist en l'esprit ses semences encloses,
   Son nom des Dieux prist l'immortalité.*

That he is thus a characteristic specimen of the poetical taste of that age, is indeed Du Bellay's chief interest. But if his work is to have the highest sort of interest, if it is to do something more than satisfy curiosity, if it is to have an æsthetic as distinct from an historical value, it is not enough for a poet to have been the true child of his age, to have conformed to its æsthetic conditions, and by so conforming have charmed and stimulated that age; it is necessary that there should be perceptible in his work something individual, inventive, unique, the impress there of the writer's own temper and personality. This impress M. Sainte-Beuve thought he found in the *Antiquités de Rome*, and the *Regrets*, which he ranks as what has been called *poésie intime*, that intensely modern sort of poetry in which the writer has for his aim the portraiture of his own most intimate moods, and to take the reader into his confidence. That age had other instances of this intimacy of sentiment; Montaigne's *Essays** are full of it, the carvings of the church of Brou are full of it. M. Sainte-Beuve has perhaps exaggerated the influence of this quality in Du Bellay's *Regrets*; but the very name of the book has a touch of Rousseau* about it, and reminds one of a whole generation of self-pitying poets in modern times. It was in the atmosphere of Rome, to him so strange and mournful, that these pale flowers grew up. For that journey to Italy, which he deplored as the greatest misfortune of his life, put him in full possession of his talent, and brought out all its originality. And in effect you do find intimacy, *intimité*, here. The trouble of his life is analysed, and the sentiment of it conveyed directly to our minds; not a great sorrow or passion, but only the sense of loss in passing days, the *ennui* of a dreamer who must plunge into the world's affairs, the opposition between actual life and the ideal, a longing for rest, nostalgia, home-sickness—that pre-eminently childish, but so suggestive sorrow, as significant of the final regret of all human creatures for the familiar earth and limited sky.

The feeling for landscape is often described as a modern one; still more so is that for antiquity, the sentiment of ruins. Du Bellay has this sentiment. The duration of the hard, sharp outlines of things is a grief to him, and passing his wearisome days among the ruins of ancient Rome, he is consoled by the thought that all must one day end, by the sentiment of the grandeur of nothingness—*la grandeur du rien*. With a strange touch of far-off mysticism, he thinks that the great whole—*le grand tout*—into which all other things pass and lose themselves, ought itself sometimes to perish and pass away. Nothing less can relieve his weariness. From the stately aspects of Rome his thoughts went back continually to France, to the smoking chimneys of his little village, the longer twilight of the north, the soft climate of Anjou—*la douceur Angevine*; yet not so much to the real France, we may be sure, with its dark streets and roofs of rough-hewn slate, as to that other country, with slenderer towers, and more winding rivers, and trees like flowers, and with softer sunshine on more gracefully-proportioned fields and ways, which the fancy of the exile, and the pilgrim, and of the schoolboy far from home, and of those kept at home unwillingly, everywhere builds up before or behind them.

He came home at last, through the *Grisons*,* by slow journeys; and there, in the cooler air of his own country, under its skies of milkier blue, the sweetest flower of his genius sprang up. There have been poets whose whole fame has rested on one poem, as Gray's on the *Elegy in a Country Churchyard*, or Ronsard's, as many critics have thought, on the eighteen lines of one famous ode.* Du Bellay has almost been the poet of one poem; and this one poem of his is an

Italian product transplanted into that green country of Anjou; out of the Latin verses of Andrea Navagero, into French. But it is a composition in which the matter is almost nothing, and the form almost everything; and the form of the poem as it stands, written in old French, is all Du Bellay's own. It is a song which the winnowers are supposed to sing as they winnow the corn, and they invoke the winds to lie lightly on the grain.

D'UN VANNEUR DE BLE AUX VENTS[1]

A vous trouppe legère
  Qui d'aile passagère
  Par le monde volez,
  Et d'un sifflant murmure
  L'ombrageuse verdure
  Doulcement esbranlez.

J'offre ces violettes,
  Ces lis & ces fleurettes,
  Et ces roses icy,
  Ces vermeillettes roses
  Sont freschement écloses,
  Et ces œlliets aussi.

De vostre doulce haleine
  Eventez ceste plaine
  Eventez ce sejour;
  Ce pendant que j'ahanne
  A mon blé que je vanne
  A la chaleur du jour.*

That has, in the highest degree, the qualities, the value, of the whole Pleiad school of poetry, of the whole phase of taste from which that school derives—a certain silvery grace of fancy, nearly all the pleasure of which is in the surprise at the happy and dexterous way in which a thing slight in itself is handled. The sweetness of it is by no means to be got at by crushing, as you crush wild herbs to get at their perfume.

---

[1] A graceful translation of this and some other poems of the *Pleiad* may be found in *Ballads and Lyrics of Old France*, by Mr. Andrew Lang.

One seems to hear the measured motion of the fans, with a child's pleasure on coming across the incident for the first time, in one of those great barns of Du Bellay's own country, *La Beauce*, the granary of France. A sudden light transfigures some trivial thing, a weather-vane, a windmill, a winnowing-fan, the dust in the barn door. A moment—and the thing has vanished, because it was pure effect; but it leaves a relish behind it, a longing that the accident may happen again.

1872.

WINCKELMANN

*ET EGO IN ARCADIA FUI**

GOETHE's fragments of art-criticism contain a few pages of strange pregnancy on the character of Winckelmann.* He speaks of the teacher who had made his career possible, but whom he had never seen, as of an abstract type of culture, consummate, tranquil, withdrawn already into the region of ideals, yet retaining colour from the incidents of a passionate intellectual life. He classes him with certain works of art, possessing an inexhaustible gift of suggestion, to which criticism may return again and again with renewed freshness. Hegel, in his lectures on the *Philosophy of Art*, estimating the work of his predecessors, has also passed a remarkable judgment on Winckelmann's writings:—'Winckelmann, by contemplation of the ideal works of the ancients, received a sort of inspiration, through which he opened a new sense for the study of art. He is to be regarded as one of those who, in the sphere of art, have known how to initiate a new organ for the human spirit.' That is has given a new sense, that it has laid open a new organ, is the highest that can be said of any critical effort. It is interesting then to ask what kind of man it was who thus laid open a new organ. Under what conditions was that effected?

Johann Joachim Winckelmann was born at Stendal, in Brandenburg, in the year 1717. The child of a poor trades-man, he passed through many struggles in early youth, the memory of which ever remained in him as a fitful cause of dejection. In 1763, in the full emancipation of his spirit, looking over the beautiful Roman prospect, he writes—'One gets spoiled here; but God owed me this; in my youth I suffered too much.' Destined to assert and interpret the charm of the Hellenic spirit, he served first a painful apprenticeship in the tarnished intellectual world of Germany in the earlier half of the eighteenth century. Passing out of that into the happy light of the antique, he had a sense of exhilaration almost physical. We find him as a child in the dusky precincts of a German school, hungrily feeding on a few colourless books. The master of this school grows blind; Winckelmann becomes his *famulus*.* The old man would have had him study theology. Winckelmann, free of the master's library, chooses rather to become familiar with the Greek classics. Herodotus and Homer win, with their 'vowelled' Greek,* his warmest enthusiasm; whole nights of fever are devoted to them; disturbing dreams of an Odyssey of his own come to him. 'He felt in himself,' says Madame de Staël, 'an ardent attraction towards the south. In German imaginations even now traces are often to be found of that love of the sun, that weariness of the north (*cette fatigue du nord*) which carried the northern peoples away into the countries of the south. A fine sky brings to birth sentiments not unlike the love of one's Fatherland.'*

To most of us, after all our steps towards it, the antique world, in spite of its intense outlines, its own perfect self-expression, still remains faint and remote. To him, closely limited except on the side of the ideal, building for his dark poverty 'a house not made with hands,'* it early came to seem more real than the present. In the fantastic plans of foreign travel continually passing through his mind, to Egypt, for instance, and to France, there seems always to be rather a wistful sense of something lost to be regained, than the desire of discovering anything new. Goethe has told us how, in his eagerness actually to handle the antique, he became interested in the insignificant vestiges of it which the neighbourhood of Strasburg afforded. So we hear of Winckelmann's boyish antiquarian wanderings among the ugly Brandenburg sandhills. Such a conformity between himself and Winckelmann, Goethe would have gladly noted.

At twenty-one he enters the University of Halle, to study theology, as his friends desire; instead, he becomes the enthusiastic translator of Herodotus, The condition of Greek learning in German schools and universities had fallen, and there were no professors at Halle who could satisfy his sharp, intellectual craving. Of his professional education he always speaks with scorn, claiming to have been his own teacher from first to last. His appointed teachers did not perceive that a new source of culture was within their hands. *Homo vagus et inconstans!**—one of them pedantically reports of the future pilgrim to Rome, unaware on which side his irony was whetted. When professional education confers nothing but irritation on a Schiller,* no one ought to be surprised; for Schiller, and such as he, are primarily spiritual adventurers. But that Winckelmann, the votary of the gravest of intellectual traditions, should get nothing but an attempt at suppression from the professional guardians of learning, is what may well surprise us.

In 1743 he became master of a school at Seehausen. This was the most wearisome period of his life. Notwithstanding a success in dealing with children, which seems to testify to something simple and primeval in his nature, he found the work of teaching very depressing. Engaged in this work, he writes that he still has within him a longing desire to attain to the knowledge of beauty—*sehnlich wünschte zur Kenntniss des Schönen zu gelangen.* He had to shorten his nights, sleeping only four hours, to gain time for reading. And here Winckelmann made a step forward in culture. He multiplied his intellectual force by detaching from it all flaccid interests. He renounced mathematics and law, in which his reading had been considerable, all but the literature of the arts. Nothing was to enter into his life unpenetrated by its central enthusiasm. At this time he undergoes the charm of Voltaire.* Voltaire belongs to that flimsier, more artificial, classical tradition, which Winckelmann was one day to supplant, by the clear ring, the eternal outline, of the genuine antique. But it proves the authority of such a gift as Voltaire's that it allures and wins even those born to supplant it. Voltaire's impression on Winckelmann was never effaced; and it gave him a consideration for French literature which contrasts with his contempt for the literary products of Germany. German literature transformed, side-realised, as we see it in Goethe, reckons Winckelmann among its initiators. But Germany at that time presented nothing in which he could have anticipated *Iphigenie,** and the formation of an effective classical tradition in German literature.

Under this purely literary influence, Winckelmann pro-
tests against Christian Wolff* and the philosophers. Goethe,
in speaking of this protest, alludes to his own obligations to
Emmanuel Kant.* Kant's influence over the culture of
Goethe, which he tells us could not have been resisted by him
without loss, consisted in a severe limitation to the concrete.
But he adds, that in born antiquaries, like Winckelmann, a
constant handling of the antique, with its eternal outline,
maintains that limitation as effectually as a critical philosophy. Plato, however, saved so often for his redeeming
literary manner, is excepted from Winckelmann's proscrip-
tion of the philosophers. The modern student most often
meets Plato on that side which seems to pass beyond Plato
into a world no longer pagan, and based upon the conception of a spiritual life. But the element of affinity which he
presents to Winckelmann is that which is wholly Greek, and
alien from the Christian world, represented by that group of
brilliant youths in the *Lysis*,* still uninfected by any spiritual
sickness, finding the end of all endeavour in the aspects of
the human form, the continual stir and motion of a comely
human life.

This new-found interest in Plato's dialogues could not fail
to increase his desire to visit the countries of the classical
tradition. 'It is my misfortune,' he writes, 'that I was not
born to great place, wherein I might have had cultivation,
and the opportunity of following my instinct and forming
myself.' A visit to Rome probably was already designed, and
he silently preparing for it. Count Bünau, the author of a
historical work then of note, had collected at Nöthenitz a
valuable library, now part of the library of Dresden. In 1784
Winckelmann wrote to Bünau in halting French:—He is
emboldened, he says, by Bünau's indulgence for needy men
of letters. He desires only to devote himself to study, having
never allowed himself to be dazzled by favourable prospects
in the Church. He hints at his doubtful position 'in a
metaphysical age, by which humane literature is trampled
under foot. At present,' he goes on, 'little value is set on
Greek literature, to which I have devoted myself so far
as I could penetrate, when good books are so scarce and

expensive.' Finally, he desires a place in some corner of Bünau's library. 'Perhaps, at some future time, I shall become more useful to the public, if, drawn from obscurity in whatever way, I can find means to maintain myself in the capital.'

Soon afterwards we find Winckelmann in the library at Nöthenitz. Thence he made many visits to the collection of antiquities at Dresden. He became acquainted with many artists, above all with Oeser,* Goethe's future friend and master, who, uniting a high culture with the practical knowledge of art, was fitted to minister to Winckelmann's culture. And now a new channel of communion with the Greek life was opened for him. Hitherto he had handled the words only of Greek poetry, stirred indeed and roused by them, yet divining beyond the words some unexpressed pulsation of sensuous life. Suddenly he is in contact with that life, still fervent in the relics of plastic art. Filled as our culture is with the classical spirit, we can hardly imagine how deeply the human mind was moved, when, at the Renaissance, in the midst of a frozen world, the buried fire of ancient art rose up from under the soil. Winckelmann here reproduces for us the earlier sentiment of the Renaissance. On a sudden the imagination feels itself free. How facile and direct, it seems to say, is this life of the senses and the understanding, when once we have apprehended it! Here, surely, is that more liberal mode of life we have been seeking so long, so near to us all the while. How mistaken and round-about have been our efforts to reach it by mystic passion, and monastic reverie; how they have deflowered the flesh; how little have they really emancipated us! Hermione melts from her stony posture, and the lost proportions of life right themselves.* Here, then, in vivid realisation, we see the native tendency of Winckelmann to escape from abstract theory to intuition, to the exercise of sight and touch. Lessing, in the *Laocoon*, has theorised finely on the relation of poetry to sculpture; and philosophy may give us theoretical reasons why not poetry but sculpture should be the most sincere and exact expression of the Greek ideal. By a happy, unperplexed dexterity, Winckelmann solves the question in the concrete. It is what Goethe calls his *Gewahrwerden der griechischen Kunst*, his *finding* of Greek art.

Through the tumultuous richness of Goethe's culture, the influence of Winckelmann is always discernible, as the strong, regulative under-current of a clear, antique motive. 'One learns nothing from him,' he says to Eckermann, 'but one becomes something.' If we ask what the secret of this influence was, Goethe himself will tell us—wholeness, unity with one's self, intellectual integrity. And yet these expressions, because they fit Goethe, with his universal culture, so well, seem hardly to describe the narrow, exclusive interest of Winckelmann. Doubtless Winckelmann's perfection is a narrow perfection: his feverish nursing of the one motive of his life is a contrast to Goethe's various energy. But what affected Goethe, what instructed him and ministered to his culture, was the integrity, the truth to its type, of the given force. The development of this force was the single interest of Winckelmann, unembarrassed by anything else in him. Other interests, practical or intellectual, those slighter talents and motives not supreme, which in most men are the waste part of nature, and drain away their vitality, he plucked out and cast from him. The protracted longing of his youth is not a vague, romantic longing: he knows what he longs for, what he wills. Within its severe limits his enthusiasm burns like lava. 'You know,' says Lavater, speaking of Winckelmann's countenance, 'that I consider ardour and indifference by no means incompatible in the same character. If ever there was a striking instance of that union, it is in the countenance before us.'* 'A lowly childhood,' says Goethe, 'insufficient instruction in youth, broken, distracted studies in early manhood, the burden of school-keeping! He was thirty years old before he enjoyed a single favour of fortune: but so soon as he had attained to an adequate condition of freedom, he appears before us consummate and entire, complete in the ancient sense.'*

But his hair is turning grey, and he has not yet reached the south. The Saxon court had become Roman Catholic, and the way to favour at Dresden was through Roman ecclesiastics. Probably the thought of a profession of the papal religion was not new to Winckelmann. At one time he had thought of begging his way to Rome, from cloister to cloister, under the pretence of a disposition to change his faith. In 1751, the papal *nuncio*, Archinto, was one of the visitors at Nöthenitz. He suggested Rome as the fitting stage for Winckelmann's accomplishments, and held out the hope of a place in the pope's library. Cardinal Passionei, charmed with Winckelmann's beautiful Greek writing, was ready to play the part of Mæcenas,* if the indispensable change were made. Winckelmann accepted the bribe, and visited the *nuncio* at Dresden. Unquiet still at the word 'profession,' not without a struggle, he joined the Roman Church, July the 11th, 1754.

Goethe boldly pleads that Winckelmann was a pagan, that the landmarks of Christendom meant nothing to him. It is clear that he intended to deceive no one by his disguise; fears of the inquisition are sometimes visible during his life in Rome; he entered Rome notoriously with the works of Voltaire in his possession; the thought of what Count Bünau might be thinking of him seems to have been his greatest difficulty. On the other hand, he may have had a sense of a certain antique and as it were pagan grandeur in the Roman Catholic religion. Turning from the crabbed Protestantism, which had been the *ennui* of his youth, he might reflect that while Rome had reconciled itself to the Renaissance, the Protestant principle in art had cut off Germany from the supreme tradition of beauty. And yet to that transparent nature, with its simplicity as of the earlier world, the loss of absolute sincerity must have been a real loss. Goethe understands that Winckelmann had made this sacrifice. Yet at the bar of the highest criticism, perhaps, Winckelmann may be absolved. The insincerity of his religious profession was only one incident of a culture in which the moral instinct, like the religious or political, was merged in the artistic. But then the artistic interest was that, by desperate faithfulness to which Winckelmann was saved from a mediocrity, which, breaking through no bounds, moves ever in a bloodless routine, and misses its one chance in the life of the spirit and the intellect. There have been instances of culture developed by every

high motive in turn, and yet intense at every point; and the
aim of our culture should be to attain not only as intense but
as complete a life as possible. But often the higher life is only
possible at all, on condition of the selection of that in which
one's motive is native and strong; and this selection involves
the renunciation of a crown reserved for others. Which is
better?—to lay open a new sense, to initiate a new organ for
the human spirit, or to cultivate many types of perfection up
to a point which leaves us still beyond the range of their
transforming power? Savonarola* is one type of success;
Winckelmann is another; criticism can reject neither, because each is true to itself. Winckelmann himself explains the
motive of his life when he says, 'It will be my highest reward,
if posterity acknowledges that I have written worthily.'

For a time he remained at Dresden. There his first book
appeared, *Thoughts on the Imitation of Greek Works of Art in
Painting and Sculpture*. Full of obscurities as it was, obscurities
which baffled but did not offend Goethe when he first turned
to art-criticism, its purpose was direct—an appeal from the
artificial classicism of the day to the study of the antique.
The book was well received, and a pension supplied through
the king's confessor. In September 1755 he started for Rome,
in the company of a young Jesuit. He was introduced to
Raphael Mengs, a painter then of note, and found a home
near him, in the artists' quarter, in a place where he could
'overlook, far and wide, the eternal city.' At first he was
perplexed with the sense of being a stranger on what was to
him, spiritually, native soil. 'Unhappily,' he cries in French,
often selected by him as the vehicle of strong feeling, 'I am
one of those whom the Greeks call ὀψιμαθεῖς.—I have come
into the world and into Italy too late.' More than thirty years
afterwards, Goethe also, after many aspirations and severe
preparation of mind, visited Italy. In early manhood, just as
he too was *finding* Greek art, the rumour of that true artist's
life of Winckelmann in Italy had strongly moved him. At
Rome, spending a whole year drawing from the antique, in
preparation for *Iphigenie*, he finds the stimulus of Winckelmann's memory ever active. Winckelmann's Roman life was
simple, primeval, Greek. His delicate constitution permitted

him the use only of bread and wine. Condemned by many as a renegade, he had no desire for places of honour, but only to see his merits acknowledged, and existence assured to him. He was simple without being niggardly; he desired to be neither poor nor rich.

Winckelmann's first years in Rome present all the elements of an intellectual situation of the highest interest. The beating of the soul against its bars, the sombre aspect, the alien traditions, the still barbarous literature of Germany, are afar off. Before him are adequate conditions of culture, the sacred soil itself, the first tokens of the advent of the new German literature, with its broad horizons, its boundless intellectual promise. Dante, passing from the darkness of the *Inferno*, is filled with a sharp and joyful sense of light, which makes him deal with it, in the opening of the *Purgatorio*, in a wonderfully touching and penetrative way. Hellenism, which is the principle pre-eminently of intellectual light, (our modern culture may have more colour, the medieval spirit greater heat and profundity, but Hellenism is pre-eminent for light,) has always been most effectively conceived by those who have crept into it out of an intellectual world in which the sombre elements predominate. So it had been in the ages of the Renaissance. This repression, removed at last, gave force and glow to Winckelmann's native affinity to the Hellenic spirit. 'There had been known before him,' says Madame de Staël, 'learned men who might be consulted like books; but no one had, if I may say so, made himself a pagan for the purpose of penetrating antiquity.' 'One is always a poor executant of conceptions not one's own.'—*On exécute mal ce qu'on n'a pas conçu soi-même*[1]—are true in their measure of every genuine enthusiasm. Enthusiasm,—that, in the broad Platonic sense of the *Phaedrus*,* was the secret of his divinatory power over the Hellenic world. This enthusiasm, dependent as it is to a great degree on bodily temperament, has a power of reinforcing the purer emotions of the intellect with an almost physical excitement. That his affinity with Hellenism was not merely intellectual,

[1] Words of Charlotte Corday* before the *Convention*.

that the subtler threads of temperament were inwoven in it, is proved by his romantic, fervent friendships with young men. He has known, he says, many young men more beautiful than Guido's archangel.* These friendships, bringing him into contact with the pride of human form, and staining the thoughts with its bloom, perfected his reconciliation to the spirit of Greek sculpture. A letter on taste, addressed from Rome to a young nobleman, Friedrich von Berg, is the record of such a friendship.

'I shall excuse my delay,' he begins, 'in fulfilling my promise of an essay on the taste for beauty in works of art, in the words of Pindar. He says to Agesidamus, a youth of Locri—ἰδέᾳ τε καλὸν, ὥρᾳ τε κεκραμένον—whom he had kept waiting for an intended ode, that a debt paid with usury is the end of reproach. This may win your good-nature on behalf of my present essay, which has turned out far more detailed and circumstantial than I had at first intended.

'It is from yourself that the subject is taken. Our intercourse has been short, too short both for you and me; but the first time I saw you, the affinity of our spirits was revealed to me: your culture proved that my hope was not groundless; and I found in a beautiful body a soul created for nobleness, gifted with the sense of beauty. My parting from you was therefore one of the most painful in my life; and that this feeling continues our common friend is witness, for your separation from me leaves me no hope of seeing you again. Let this essay be a memorial of our friendship, which, on my side, is free from every selfish motive, and ever remains subject and dedicate to yourself alone.'

The following passage is characteristic—

'As it is confessedly the beauty of man which is to be conceived under one general idea, so I have noticed that those who are observant of beauty only in women, and are moved little or not at all by the beauty of men, seldom have an impartial, vital, inborn instinct for beauty in art. To such persons the beauty of Greek art will ever seem wanting, because its supreme beauty is rather male than female. But the beauty of art demands a higher sensibility than the beauty of nature, because the beauty of art, like tears shed at a play, gives no pain, is without life, and must be awakened and repaired by culture. Now, as the spirit of culture is much more ardent in youth than in manhood, the instinct of which I am speaking must be exercised and directed to what is beautiful, before that age is reached, at which one would be afraid to confess that one had no taste for it.'

Certainly, of that beauty of living form which regulated Winckelmann's friendships, it could not be said that it gave no pain. One notable friendship, the fortune of which we may trace through his letters, begins with an antique, chivalrous letter in French, and ends noisily in a burst of angry fire. Far from reaching the quietism, the bland indifference of art, such attachments are nevertheless more susceptible than any others of equal strength of a purely intellectual culture. Of passion, of physical excitement, they contain only just so much as stimulates the eye to the finest delicacies of colour and form. These friendships, often the caprices of a moment, make Winckelmann's letters, with their troubled colouring, an instructive but bizarre addition to the *History of Art*, that shrine of grave and mellow light around the mute Olympian family. The impression which Winckelmann's literary life conveyed to those about him, was that of excitement, intuition, inspiration, rather than the contemplative evolution of general principles. The quick, susceptible enthusiast, betraying his temperament even in appearance, by his olive complexion, his deep-seated, piercing eyes, his rapid movements, apprehended the subtlest principles of the Hellenic manner, not through the understanding, but by instinct or touch. A German biographer of Winckelmann has compared him to Columbus. That is not the aptest of comparisons; but it reminds one of a passage in which Edgar Quinet* describes the great discoverer's famous voyage. His science was often at fault; but he had a way of estimating at once the slightest indication of land, in a floating weed or passing bird; he seemed actually to come nearer to nature than other men. And that world in which others had moved with so much embarrassment, seems to call out in Winckelmann new senses fitted to deal with it. He is in touch with it; it penetrates him, and becomes part of his

temperament. He remodels his writings with constant re-
newal of insight; he catches the thread of a whole sequence
of laws in some hollowing of the hand, or dividing of the
hair; he seems to realise that fancy of the reminiscence of a
forgotten knowledge hidden for a time in the mind itself; as
if the mind of one, lover and philosopher at once in some
phase of pre-existence—φιλοσοφήσας πότε μέτ᾽ ἔρωτος—
fallen into a new cycle, were beginning its intellectual career
over again, yet with a certain power of anticipating its
results. And so comes the truth of Goethe's judgments on his
works; they are a life, a living thing, designed for those who
are alive—*ein Lebendiges für die Lebendigen geschrieben, ein Leben
selbst.*

In 1758 Cardinal Albani, who had formed in his Roman
villa a precious collection of antiquities, became Winckelmann's patron. Pompeii had just opened its treasures;
Winckelmann gathered its first-fruits. But his plan of a visit
to Greece remained unfulfilled. From his first arrival in
Rome he had kept the *History of Ancient Art* ever in view. All
his other writings were a preparation for that. It appeared,
finally, in 1764; but even after its publication Winckelmann
was still employed in perfecting it. It is since his time that
many of the most significant examples of Greek art have
been submitted to criticism. He had seen little or nothing of
what we ascribe to the age of Pheidias;* and his conception
of Greek art tends, therefore, to put the mere elegance of the
imperial society of ancient Rome in place of the severe and
chastened grace of the *palaestra.** For the most part he had to
penetrate to Greek art through copies, imitations, and later
Roman art itself; and it is not surprising that this turbid
medium has left in Winckelmann's actual results much that
a more privileged criticism can correct.

He had been twelve years in Rome. Admiring Germany
had made many calls to him. At last, in 1768, he set out to
revisit the country of his birth; and as he left Rome, a
strange, inverted home-sickness, a strange reluctance to
leave it at all, came over him. He reached Vienna. There he
was loaded with honours and presents: other cities were
awaiting him. Goethe, then nineteen years old, studying art

at Leipsic, was expecting his coming, with that wistful eagerness which marked his youth, when the news of Winckelmann's murder arrived. All his 'weariness of the north' had revived with double force. He left Vienna, intending to hasten back to Rome, and at Trieste a delay of a few days occurred. With characteristic openness, Winckelmann had confided his plans to a fellow-traveller, a man named Arcangeli, and had shown him the gold medals received at Vienna. Arcangeli's avarice was roused. One morning he entered Winckelmann's room, under pretence of taking leave. Winckelmann was then writing 'memoranda for the future editor of the *History of Art*,' still seeking the perfection of his great work. Arcangeli begged to see the medals once more. As Winckelmann stooped down to take them from the chest, a cord was thrown round his neck. Some time afterwards, a child with whose companionship Winckelmann had beguiled his delay, knocked at the door, and receiving no answer, gave the alarm. Winckelmann was found dangerously wounded, and died a few hours later, after receiving the last sacraments. It seemed as if the gods, in reward for his devotion to them, had given him a death which, for its swiftness and its opportunity, he might well have desired. 'He has,' says Goethe, 'the advantage of figuring in the memory of posterity, as one eternally able and strong; for the image in which one leaves the world, is that in which one moves among the shadows.' Yet, perhaps, it is not fanciful to regret that his proposed meeting with Goethe never took place. Goethe, then in all the pregnancy of his wonderful youth, still unruffled by the 'press and storm' of his earlier manhood, was awaiting Winckelmann with a curiosity of the worthiest kind. As it was, Winckelmann became to him something like what Virgil was to Dante. And Winckelmann, with his fiery friendships, had reached that age and that period of culture at which emotions hitherto fitful, sometimes concentrate themselves in a vital, unchangeable relationship. German literary history seems to have lost the chance of one of those famous friendships, the very tradition of which becomes a stimulus to culture, and exercises an imperishable influence.

In one of the frescoes of the Vatican, Raphael has commemorated the tradition of the Catholic religion. Against a space of tranquil sky, broken in upon by the beatific vision, are ranged the great personages of Christian history, with the Sacrament in the midst. Another fresco* of Raphael in the same apartment presents a very different company, Dante alone appearing in both. Surrounded by the muses of Greek mythology, under a thicket of laurel, sits Apollo, with the sources of Castalia* at his feet. On either side are grouped those on whom the spirit of Apollo descended, the classical and Renaissance poets, to whom the waters of Castalia come down, a river making glad this other 'City of God.'* In this fresco it is the classical tradition, the orthodoxy of taste, that Raphael commemorates. Winckelmann's intellectual history authenticates the claims of this tradition in human culture. In the countries where that tradition arose, where it still lurked about its own artistic relics, and changes of language had not broken its continuity, national pride might sometimes light up anew an enthusiasm for it. Aliens might imitate that enthusiasm, and classicism become from time to time an intellectual fashion. But Winckelmann was not further removed by language, than by local aspects and associations, from those vestiges of the classical spirit; and he lived at a time when, in Germany, classical studies were out of favour. Yet, remote in time and place, he feels after the Hellenic world, divines those channels of ancient art, in which its life still circulates, and, like Scyles, the half-barbarous yet Hellenising king, in the beautiful story of Herodotus,* is irresistibly attracted by it. This testimony to the authority of the Hellenic tradition, its fitness to satisfy some vital requirement of the intellect, which Winckelmann contributes as a solitary man of genius, is offered also by the general history of the mind. The spiritual forces of the past, which have prompted and informed the culture of a succeeding age, live, indeed, within that culture, but with an absorbed, underground life. The Hellenic element alone has not been so absorbed, or content with this underground life; from time to time it has started to the surface; culture has been drawn back to its sources to be clarified and corrected. Hellenism is not merely an absorbed element in our intellectual life; it is a conscious tradition in it.

Again, individual genius works ever under conditions of time and place: its products are coloured by the varying aspects of nature, and type of human form, and outward manners of life. There is thus an element of change in art; criticism must never for a moment forget that 'the artist is the child of his time.' But besides these conditions of time and place, and independent of them, there is also an element of permanence, a standard of taste, which genius confesses. This standard is maintained in a purely intellectual tradition. It acts upon the artist, not as one of the influences of his own age, but through those artistic products of the previous generation which first excited, while they directed into a particular channel, his sense of beauty. The supreme artistic products of succeeding generations thus form a series of elevated points, taking each from each the reflexion of a strange light, the source of which is not in the atmosphere around and above them, but in a stage of society remote from ours. The standard of taste, then, was fixed in Greece, at a definite historical period. A tradition for all succeeding generations, it originates in a spontaneous growth out of the influences of Greek society. What were the conditions under which this ideal, this standard of artistic orthodoxy, was generated? How was Greece enabled to force its thought upon Europe?

Greek art, when we first catch sight of it, is entangled with Greek religion. We are accustomed to think of Greek religion as the religion of art and beauty, the religion of which the Olympian Zeus and the Athene Polias* are the idols, the poems of Homer the sacred books. Thus Cardinal Newman speaks of 'the classical polytheism which was gay and graceful, as was natural in a civilised age.'* Yet such a view is only a partial one. In it the eye is fixed on the sharp, bright edge of high Hellenic culture, but loses sight of the sombre world across which it strikes. Greek religion, where we can observe it most distinctly, is at once a magnificent ritualistic system, and a cycle of poetical conceptions. Religions, as they grow by natural laws out of man's life, are modified by whatever modifies his life. They brighten under a bright sky, they become liberal as the social range widens, they grow intense and shrill in the clefts of human life, where the spirit is narrow and confined, and the stars are visible at noonday; and a fine analysis of these differences is one of the gravest functions of religious criticism. Still, the broad foundation, in mere human nature, of all religions as they exist for the greatest number, is a universal pagan sentiment, a paganism which existed before the Greek religion, and has lingered far onward into the Christian world, ineradicable, like some persistent vegetable growth, because its seed is an element of the very soil out of which it springs.

This pagan sentiment measures the sadness with which the human mind is filled, whenever its thoughts wander far from what is here, and now. It is beset by notions of irresistible natural powers, for the most part ranged against man, but the secret also of his fortune, making the earth golden and the grape fiery for him. He makes gods in his own image, gods smiling and flower-crowned, or bleeding by some sad fatality, to console him by their wounds, never closed from generation to generation. It is with a rush of home-sickness that the thought of death presents itself. He would remain at home for ever on the earth if he could. As it loses its colour and the senses fail, he clings ever closer to it; but since the mouldering of bones and flesh must go on to the end, he is careful for charms and talismans, which may chance to have some friendly power in them, when the inevitable shipwreck comes. Such sentiment is a part of the eternal basis of all religions, modified indeed by changes of time and place, but indestructible, because its root is so deep in the earth of man's nature. The breath of religious initiators passes over them; a few 'rise up with wings as eagles,'* but the broad level of religious life is not permanently changed. Religious progress, like all purely spiritual progress, is confined to a few. This sentiment attaches itself in the earliest times to certain usages of patriarchal life, the kindling of fire, the washing of the body, the slaughter of the flock, the gathering of harvest, holidays and dances. Here are the beginnings of a ritual, at first as occasional and unfixed as the sentiment

which it expresses, but destined to become the permanent
element of religious life. The usages of patriarchal life
change; but this germ of ritual remains, promoted now with
a consciously religious motive, losing its domestic character,
and therefore becoming more and more inexplicable with
each generation. Such pagan worship, in spite of local
variations, essentially one, is an element in all religions. It is
the anodyne which the religious principle, like one adminis-
tering opiates to the incurable, has added to the law which
makes life sombre for the vast majority of mankind.

More definite religious conceptions come from other
sources, and fix themselves upon this ritual in various ways,
changing it, and giving it new meanings. In Greece they
were derived from mythology, itself not due to a religious
source at all, but developing in the course of time into a body
of religious conceptions, entirely human in form and character. To the unprogressive ritual element it brought these
conceptions, itself—ἡ πτεροῦ δύναμις, the power of the
wing*—an element of refinement, of ascension, with the
promise of an endless destiny. While the ritual remains
unchanged, the æsthetic element, only accidentally connected with it, expands with the freedom and mobility of the
things of the intellect. Always, the fixed element is the
religious observance; the fluid, unfixed element is the myth,
the religious conception. This religion is itself pagan, and has
in any broad view of it the pagan sadness. It does not at
once, and for the majority, become the higher Hellenic
religion. The country people, of course, cherish the unlovely
idols of an earlier time, such as those which Pausanias*
found still devoutly preserved in Arcadia. Athenæus* tells
the story of one who, coming to a temple of Latona, had
expected to find some worthy presentment of the mother of
Apollo, and laughed on seeing only a shapeless wooden
figure. The wilder people have wilder gods, which, however,
in Athens, or Corinth, or Lacedæmon, changing ever with
the worshippers in whom they live and move and have their
being, borrow something of the lordliness and distinction of
human nature there. Greek religion too has its mendicants,
its purifications, its antinomian mysticism, its garments

offered to the gods, its statues worn with kissing, its exaggerated superstitions for the vulgar only, its worship of sorrow,
its *addolorata*,* its mournful mysteries. Scarcely a wild or
melancholy note of the medieval church but was anticipated
by Greek polytheism! What should we have thought of the
vertiginous prophetess at the very centre of Greek religion?
The supreme Hellenic culture is a sharp edge of light across
this gloom. The fiery, stupefying wine becomes in a happier
climate clear and exhilarating. The Dorian worship of
Apollo, rational, chastened, debonair, with his unbroken
daylight, always opposed to the sad Chthonian divinities,* is
the aspiring element, by force and spring of which Greek
religion sublimes itself. Out of Greek religion, under happy
conditions, arises Greek art, to minister to human culture. It
was the privilege of Greek religion to be able to transform
itself into an artistic ideal.

For the thoughts of the Greeks about themselves, and their
relation to the world generally, were ever in the happiest
readiness to be transformed into objects for the senses. In this
lies the main distinction between Greek art and the mystical
art of the Christian middle age, which is always struggling to
express thoughts beyond itself. Take, for instance, a characteristic work of the middle age, Angelico's* *Coronation of the
Virgin*, in the cloister of *Saint Mark's* at Florence. In some
strange halo of a moon Jesus and the Virgin Mother are
seated, clad in mystical white raiment, half shroud, half
priestly linen. Jesus, with rosy nimbus and the long pale
hair—*tanquam lana alba et tanquam nix**—of the figure in the
Apocalypse, with slender finger-tips is setting a crown of
pearl on the head of Mary, who, corpse-like in her refinement, is bending forward to receive it, the light lying like
snow upon her forehead. Certainly, it cannot be said of
Angelico's fresco that it throws into a sensible form our
highest thoughts about man and his relation to the world;
but it did not do this adequately even for Angelico. For him,
all that is outward or sensible in his work—the hair like wool,
the rosy nimbus, the crown of pearl—is only the symbol or
type of a really inexpressible world, to which he wishes to
direct the thoughts; he would have shrunk from the notion

that what the eye apprehended was all. Such forms of art, then, are inadequate to the matter they clothe; they remain ever below its level. Something of this kind is true also of oriental art. As in the middle age from an exaggerated inwardness, so in the East from a vagueness, a want of definition, in thought, the matter presented to art is unmanageable, and the forms of sense struggle vainly with it. The many-headed gods of the East, the orientalised, many-breasted Diana of Ephesus,* like Angelico's fresco, are at best overcharged symbols, a means of hinting at an idea which art cannot fitly or completely express, which still remains in the world of shadows.

But take a work of Greek art,—the Venus of Melos.* That is in no sense a symbol, a suggestion, of anything beyond its own victorious fairness. The mind begins and ends with the finite image, yet loses no part of the spiritual motive. This motive is not lightly and loosely attached to the sensuous form, as its meaning to an allegory, but saturates and is identical with it. The Greek mind had advanced to a particular stage of self-reflexion, but was careful not to pass beyond it. In oriental thought there is a vague conception of life everywhere, but no true appreciation of itself by the mind, no knowledge of the distinction of man's nature: in its consciousness of itself, humanity is still confused with the fantastic, indeterminate life of the animal and vegetable world. In Greek thought, on the other hand, the 'lordship of the soul' is recognised; that lordship gives authority and divinity to human eyes and hands and feet; inanimate nature is thrown into the background. But just there Greek thought finds its happy limit; it has not yet become too inward; the mind has not yet learned to boast its independence of the flesh; the spirit has not yet absorbed everything with its emotions, nor reflected its own colour everywhere. It has indeed committed itself to a train of reflexion which must end in defiance of form, of all that is outward, in an exaggerated idealism. But that end is still distant; it has not yet plunged into the depths of religious mysticism.

This ideal art, in which the thought does not outstrip or lie beyond the proper range of its sensible embodiment, could not have arisen out of a phase of life that was uncomely or poor. That delicate pause in Greek reflexion was joined, by some supreme good luck, to the perfect animal nature of the Greeks. Here are the two conditions of an artistic ideal. The influences which perfected the animal nature of the Greeks are part of the process by which 'the ideal' was evolved. Those 'Mothers' who, in the second part of *Faust*, mould and remould the typical forms that appear in human history, preside, at the beginning of Greek culture, over such a concourse of happy physical conditions as ever generates by natural laws some rare type of intellectual or spiritual life. That delicate air, 'nimbly and sweetly recommending itself'* to the senses, the finer aspects of nature, the finer lime and clay of the human form, and modelling of the dainty framework of the human countenance:—these are the good luck of the Greek when he enters upon life. Beauty becomes a distinction, like genius, or noble place.

'By no people,' says Winckelmann, 'has beauty been so highly esteemed as by the Greeks. The priests of a youthful Jupiter at Ægæ, of the Ismenian Apollo, and the priest who at Tanagra led the procession of Mercury, bearing a lamb upon his shoulders, were always youths to whom the prize of beauty had been awarded. The citizens of Egesta erected a monument to a certain Philip who was not their fellow-citizen, but of Croton, for his distinguished beauty; and the people made offerings at it. In an ancient song, ascribed to Simonides or Epicharmus, of four wishes, the first was health, the second beauty. And as beauty was so longed for and prized by the Greeks, every beautiful person sought to become known to the whole people by this distinction, and above all to approve himself to the artists, because they awarded the prize; and this was for the artists an occasion for having supreme beauty ever before their eyes. Beauty even gave a right to fame; and we find in Greek histories the most beautiful people distinguished. Some were famous for the beauty of one single part of their form; as Demetrius Phalereus, for his beautiful eyebrows, was called *Charito-blepharos*. It seems even to have been thought that the procreation of beautiful children might be promoted by prizes. This is shown by the existence of contests for beauty, which in ancient times were established by Cypselus, King of Arcadia, by the river Alpheus; and, at the feast of Apollo of Philæ, a prize was offered to the youths for the deftest kiss. This was decided by an umpire; as also at Megara, by the grave of Diocles. At Sparta, and at Lesbos, in the temple of Juno, and among the Parrhasii, there were contests for beauty among women. The general esteem for beauty went so far, that the Spartan women set up in their bedchambers a Nireus, a Narcissus, or a Hyacinth, that they might bear beautiful children.'

So, from a few stray antiquarianisms, a few faces cast up sharply from the waves, Winckelmann, as his manner was, divines the temperament of the antique world, and that in which it had delight. It has passed away with that distant age, and we may venture to dwell upon it. What sharpness and reality it has is the sharpness and reality of suddenly arrested life. The Greek system of gymnastics originated as part of a religious ritual. The worshipper was to recommend himself to the gods by becoming fleet and fair, white and red, like them. The beauty of the *palaestra*,* and the beauty of the artist's workshop, reacted on one another. The youth tried to rival his gods; and his increased beauty passed back into them.—'I take the gods to witness, I had rather have a fair body than a king's crown'—Ὄμνυμι πάντας θεοὺς μὴ ἑλέσθαι ἂν τὴν βασιλέως ἀρχὴν ἀντὶ τοῦ καλὸς εἶναι*—that is the form in which one age of the world chose the higher life.—A perfect world, if the gods could have seemed for ever only fleet and fair, white and red! Let us not regret that this unperplexed youth of humanity, satisfied with the vision of itself, passed, at the due moment, into a mournful maturity; for already the deep joy was in store for the spirit, of finding the ideal of that youth still red with life in the grave.

It followed that the Greek ideal expressed itself pre-eminently in sculpture. All art has a sensuous element, colour, form, sound—in poetry a dexterous recalling of these, together with the profound, joyful sensuousness of motion, and each of them may be a medium for the ideal: it is partly accident which in any individual case makes the born artist, poet, or painter rather than sculptor. But as the mind itself has had an historical development, one form of art, by the very limitations of its material, may be more adequate than another for the expression of any one phase of that development. Different attitudes of the imagination have a native affinity with different types of sensuous form, so that they combine together, with completeness and ease. The arts may thus be ranged in a series, which corresponds to a series of developments in the human mind itself. Architecture, which begins in a practical need, can only express by vague hint or symbol, the spirit or mind of the artist. He closes his sadness over him, or wanders in the perplexed intricacies of things, or projects his purpose from him clean-cut and sincere, or bares himself to the sunlight. But these spiritualities, felt rather than seen, can but lurk about architectural form as volatile effects, to be gathered from it by reflexion. Their expression is, indeed, not really sensuous at all. As human form is not the subject with which it deals, architecture is the mode in which the artistic effort centres, when the thoughts of man concerning himself are still indistinct, when he is still little preoccupied with those harmonies, storms, victories, of the unseen and intellectual world, which, wrought out into the bodily form, give it an interest and significance communicable to it alone. The art of Egypt, with its supreme architectural effects, is, according to Hegel's beautiful comparison, a Memnon waiting for the day,* the day of the Greek spirit, the humanistic spirit, with its power of speech.

Again, painting, music, and poetry, with their endless power of complexity, are the special arts of the romantic and modern ages. Into these, with the utmost attenuation of detail, may be translated every delicacy of thought and feeling, incidental to a consciousness brooding with delight over itself. Through their gradations of shade, their exquisite intervals, they project in an external form that which is most inward in passion or sentiment. Between architecture and those romantic arts of painting, music, and poetry, comes sculpture, which, unlike architecture, deals immediately with man, while it contrasts with the romantic arts, because it is not self-analytical. It has to do more exclusively than any other art with the human form, itself one entire medium of spiritual expression, trembling, blushing, melting into dew, with inward excitement. That spirituality which only lurks about architecture as a volatile effect, in sculpture takes up the whole given material, and penetrates it with an imaginative motive; and at first sight sculpture, with its solidity of form, seems a thing more real and full than the faint, abstract world of poetry or painting. Still the fact is the reverse. Discourse and action show man as he is, more directly than the play of the muscles and the moulding of the flesh; and over these poetry has command. Painting, by the flushing of colour in the face and dilatation of light in the eye—music, by its subtle range of tones—can refine most delicately upon a single moment of passion, unravelling its subtlest threads.

But why should sculpture thus limit itself to pure form? Because, by this limitation, it becomes a perfect medium of expression for one peculiar motive of the imaginative intellect. It therefore renounces all those attributes of its material which do not forward that motive. It has had, indeed, from the beginning an unfixed claim to colour; but this element of colour in it has always been more or less conventional, with no melting or modulation of tones, never permitting more than a very limited realism. It was maintained chiefly as a religious tradition. In proportion as the art of sculpture ceased to be merely decorative, and subordinate to architecture, it threw itself upon pure form. It renounces the power of expression by lower or heightened tones. In it, no member of the human form is more significant than the rest; the eye is wide, and without pupil; the lips and brow are hardly less significant than hands, and breasts, and feet. But the limitation of its resources is part of its pride: it has no backgrounds, no sky or atmosphere, to suggest and interpret a train of feeling; a little of suggested motion, and much of pure light on its gleaming surfaces, with pure form—only these. And it gains more than it loses by this limitation to its own distinguishing motives; it unveils man in the repose of his unchanging characteristics. That white light purged from the angry, bloodlike stains of action and passion, reveals, not what is accidental in man, but the tranquil godship in him, as opposed to the restless accidents of life. The art of sculpture records the first naïve, unperplexed recognition of man by himself; and it is a proof of the high artistic capacity of the Greeks, that they apprehended and remained true to these exquisite limitations, yet, in spite of them, gave to their creations a mobile, a vital, individuality.

Heiterkeit—blitheness or repose, and *Allgemeinheit**—generality or breadth, are, then, the supreme characteristics of the Hellenic ideal. But that generality or breadth has nothing in common with the lax observation, the unlearned thought, the flaccid execution, which have sometimes claimed superiority in art, on the plea of being 'broad' or 'general.' Hellenic breadth and generality come of a culture minute, severe, constantly renewed, rectifying and concentrating its impressions into certain pregnant types.

The basis of all artistic genius lies in the power of conceiving humanity in a new and striking way, of putting a happy world of its own creation in place of the meaner world of our common days, generating around itself an atmosphere with a novel power of refraction, selecting, transforming, recombining the images it transmits, according to choice of the imaginative intellect. In exercising this power, painting and poetry have a variety of subject almost unlimited. The range of characters or persons open to them is as various as life itself; no character, however trivial, misshapen, or unlovely, can resist their magic. That is because those arts can accomplish their function in the choice and development of some special situation, which lifts or glorifies a character, in itself not poetical. To realise this situation, to define, in a chill and empty atmosphere, the focus where rays, in themselves pale and impotent, unite and begin to burn, the artist may have, indeed, to employ the most cunning detail, to complicate and refine upon thought and passion a thousand-fold. Let us take a brilliant example from the poems of Robert Browning. His poetry is pre-eminently the poetry of situations. The characters themselves are always of secondary importance; often they are characters in themselves of little interest; they seem to come to him by strange accidents from the ends of the world. His gift is shown by the way in which he accepts such a character, throws it into some situation, or apprehends it in some delicate pause of life, in which for a moment it becomes ideal. In the poem entitled *Le Byron de nos Jours*, in his *Dramatis Personae*,* we have a single moment of passion thrown into relief after this exquisite fashion. Those two jaded Parisians are not intrinsically interesting: they begin to interest us only when thrown into a choice situation. But to discriminate that moment, to make it appreciable by us, that we may 'find' it, what a cobweb of allusions, what double and treble reflexions of the mind upon itself, what an artificial light is constructed and broken over the chosen situation: on how fine a needle's point that little world of passion is balanced! Yet, in spite of this intricacy, the poem has the clear ring of a central motive. We receive from it the impression of one imaginative tone, of a single creative act.

To produce such effects at all requires all the resources of painting, with its power of indirect expression, of subordinate but significant detail, its atmosphere, its foregrounds and backgrounds. To produce them in a pre-eminent degree requires all the resources of poetry, language in its most purged form, its remote associations and suggestions, its double and treble lights. These appliances sculpture cannot command. In it, therefore, not the special situation, but the type, the general character of the subject to be delineated, is all-important. In poetry and painting, the situation predominates over the character; in sculpture, the character over the situation. Excluded by the proper limitation of its material from the development of exquisite situations, it has to choose from a select number of types intrinsically interesting— interesting, that is, independently of any special situation into which they may be thrown. Sculpture finds the secret of its power in presenting these types, in their broad, central, incisive lines. This it effects not by accumulation of detail, but by abstracting from it. All that is accidental, all that distracts the simple effect upon us of the supreme types of humanity, all traces in them of the commonness of the world, it gradually purges away.

Works of art produced under this law, and only these, are really characterised by Hellenic generality or breadth. In every direction it is a law of restraint. It keeps passion always below that degree of intensity at which it must necessarily be transitory, never winding up the features to one note of anger, or desire, or surprise. In some of the feebler allegorical designs of the middle age, we find isolated qualities portrayed as by so many masks; its religious art has familiarised us with faces fixed immovably into blank types of placid reverie. Men and women, again, in the hurry of life, often wear the sharp impress of one absorbing motive, from which it is said death sets their features free. All such instances may be ranged under the *grotesque*; and the Hellenic ideal has nothing in common with the grotesque. It allows passion to play lightly over the surface of the individual form, losing thereby nothing of its central impassivity, its depth and repose. To all but the highest culture, the reserved faces of the gods will ever have something of insipidity.

Again, in the best Greek sculpture, the archaic immobility has been stirred, its forms are in motion; but it is a motion ever kept in reserve, and very seldom committed to any definite action. Endless as are the attitudes of Greek sculpture, exquisite as is the invention of the Greeks in this direction, the actions or situations it permits are simple and few. There is no Greek Madonna; the goddesses are always childless. The actions selected are those which would be without significance, except in a divine person—binding on a sandal, or preparing for the bath. When a more complex and significant action is permitted, it is most often represented as just finished, so that eager expectancy is excluded, as in the image of Apollo just after the slaughter of the Python,* or of Venus with the apple of Paris already in her hand.* The *Laocoon*,* with all that patient science through which it has triumphed over an almost unmanageable subject, marks a period in which sculpture has begun to aim at effects legitimate, because delightful, only in painting.

The hair, so rich a source of expression in painting,

because, relatively to the eye or the lip, it is mere drapery, is withdrawn from attention; its texture, as well as its colour, is lost, its arrangement but faintly and severely indicated, with no broken or enmeshed light. The eyes are wide and directionless, not fixing anything with their gaze, nor riveting the brain to any special external object, the brows without hair. Again, Greek sculpture deals almost exclusively with youth, where the moulding of the bodily organs is still as if suspended between growth and completion, indicated but not emphasised; where the transition from curve to curve is so delicate and elusive, that Winckelmann compares it to a quiet sea, which, although we understand it to be in motion, we nevertheless regard as an image of repose; where, therefore, the exact degree of development is so hard to apprehend. If a single product only of Hellenic art were to be saved in the wreck of all beside, one might choose perhaps from the 'beautiful multitude' of the Panathenaic frieze,* that line of youths on horseback, with their level glances, their proud, patient lips, their chastened reins, their whole bodies in exquisite service. This colourless, unclassified purity of life, with its blending and interpenetration of intellectual, spiritual, and physical elements, still folded together, pregnant with the possibilities of a whole world closed within it, is the highest expression of the indifference which lies beyond all that is relative or partial. Everywhere there is the effect of an awaking, of a child's sleep just disturbed. All these effects are united in a single instance—the *adorante** of the museum of Berlin, a youth who has gained the wrestler's prize, with hands lifted and open, in praise for the victory. Fresh, unperplexed, it is the image of man as he springs first from the sleep of nature, his white light taking no colour from any one-sided experience. He is characterless, so far as *character* involves subjection to the accidental influences of life.

'This sense', says Hegel,* 'for the consummate modelling of divine and human forms was pre-eminently at home in Greece. In its poets and orators, its historians and philosophers, Greece cannot be conceived from a central point, unless one brings, as a key to the understanding of it, an

insight into the ideal forms of sculpture, and regards the
images of statesmen and philosophers, as well as epic and
dramatic heroes, from the artistic point of view. For those
who act, as well as those who create and think, have, in those
beautiful days of Greece, this plastic character. They are
great and free, and have grown up on the soil of their own
individuality, creating themselves out of themselves, and
moulding themselves to what they were, and willed to be.
The age of Pericles was rich in such characters; Pericles
himself, Pheidias, Plato, above all Sophocles, Thucydides
also, Xenophon and Socrates, each in his own order, the
perfection of one remaining undiminished by that of the
others. They are ideal artists of themselves, cast each in one
flawless mould, works of art, which stand before us as an
immortal presentment of the gods. Of this modelling also are
those bodily works of art, the victors in the Olympic games;
yes! and even Phryne, who, as the most beautiful of women,
ascended naked out of the water, in the presence of assem-
bled Greece.'

This key to the understanding of the Greek spirit, Winckelmann possessed in his own nature, itself like a relic of
classical antiquity, laid open by accident to our alien,
modern atmosphere. To the criticism of that consummate
Greek modelling he brought not only his culture but his
temperament. We have seen how definite was the leading
motive of that culture; how, like some central root-fibre, it
maintained the well-rounded unity of his life through a
thousand distractions. Interests not his, nor meant for him,
never disturbed him. In morals, as in criticism, he followed
the clue of instinct, of an unerring instinct. Penetrating into
the antique world by his passion, his temperament, he
enunciated no formal principles, always hard and one-sided.
Minute and anxious as his culture was, he never became one-
sidedly self-analytical. Occupied ever with himself, perfecting himself and developing his genius, he was not content, as
so often happens with such natures, that the atmosphere
between him and other minds should be thick and clouded;
he was ever jealously refining his meaning into a form,
express, clear, objective. This temperament he nurtured and

invigorated by friendships which kept him always in direct contact with the spirit of youth. The beauty of the Greek statues was a sexless beauty: the statues of the gods had the least traces of sex. Here there is a moral sexlessness, a kind of ineffectual wholeness of nature, yet with a true beauty and significance of its own.

One result of this temperament is a serenity—*Heiterkeit*— which characterises Winckelmann's handling of the sensuous side of Greek art. This serenity is, perhaps, in great measure, a negative quality: it is the absence of any sense of want, or corruption, or shame. With the sensuous element in Greek art he deals in the pagan manner; and what is implied in that? It has been sometimes said that art is a means of escape from 'the tyranny of the senses.' It may be so for the spectator: he may find that the spectacle of supreme works of art takes from the life of the senses something of its turbid fever. But this is possible for the spectator only because the artist, in producing those works, has gradually sunk his intellectual and spiritual ideas in sensuous form. He may live, as Keats lived, a pure life; but his soul, like that of Plato's false astronomer,* becomes more and more immersed in sense, until nothing which lacks the appeal to sense has interest for him. How could such an one ever again endure the greyness of the ideal or spiritual world? The spiritualist is satisfied as he watches the escape of the sensuous elements from his conceptions; his interest grows, as the dyed garment bleaches in the keener air. But the artist steeps his thought again and again into the fire of colour. To the Greek this immersion in the sensuous was, religiously, at least, indifferent. Greek sensuousness, therefore, does not fever the conscience: it is shameless and childlike. Christian asceticism, on the other hand, discrediting the slightest touch of sense, has from time to time provoked into strong emphasis the contrast or antagonism to itself, of the artistic life, with its inevitable sensuousness.—*I did but taste a little honey with the end of the rod that was in mine hand, and lo! I must die.*— It has sometimes seemed hard to pursue that life without something of conscious disavowal of a spiritual world; and this imparts to genuine artistic interests a kind of intoxication. From this intoxication Winckelmann is free: he fingers those pagan marbles with unsinged hands, with no sense of shame or loss. That is to deal with the sensuous side of art in the pagan manner.

The longer we contemplate that Hellenic ideal, in which man is at unity with himself, with his physical nature, with the outward world, the more we may be inclined to regret that he should ever have passed beyond it, to contend for a perfection that makes the blood turbid, and frets the flesh, and discredits the actual world about us. But if he was to be saved from the *ennui* which ever attaches itself to realisation, even the realisation of the perfect life, it was necessary that a conflict should come, that some sharper note should grieve the existing harmony, and the spirit chafed by it beat out at last only a larger and profounder music. In Greek tragedy this conflict has begun: man finds himself face to face with rival claims. Greek tragedy shows how such a conflict may be treated with serenity, how the evolution of it may be a spectacle of the dignity, not of the impotence, of the human spirit. But it is not only in tragedy that the Greek spirit showed itself capable of thus bringing joy out of matter in itself full of discouragements. Theocritus* too strikes often a note of romantic sadness. But what a blithe and steady poise, above these discouragements, in a clear and sunny stratum of the air!

Into this stage of Greek achievement Winckelmann did not enter. Supreme as he is where his true interest lay, his insight into the typical unity and repose of the highest sort of sculpture seems to have involved limitation in another direction. His conception of art excludes that bolder type of it which deals confidently and serenely with life, conflict, evil. Living in a world of exquisite but abstract and colour- less form, he could hardly have conceived of the subtle and penetrative, yet somewhat grotesque art of the modern world. What would he have thought of Gilliatt, in Victor Hugo's *Travailleurs de la Mer*, or of the bleeding mouth of Fantine in the first part of *Les Misérables*,* penetrated as those books are with a sense of beauty, as lively and transparent as that of a Greek? Nay, a sort of preparation for the romantic temper is noticeable even within the limits of the Greek ideal itself, which for his part Winckelmann failed to see. For Greek religion has not merely its mournful mysteries of Adonis,* of Hyacinthus,* of Demeter,* but it is conscious also of the fall of earlier divine dynasties. Hyperion* gives way to Apollo, Oceanus* to Poseidon. Around the feet of that tranquil Olympian family still crowd the weary shadows of an earlier, more formless, divine world. The placid minds even of Olympian gods are troubled with thoughts of a limit to duration, of inevitable decay, of dispossession. Again, the supreme and colourless abstraction of those divine forms, which is the secret of their repose, is also a premonition of the fleshless, consumptive refinements of the pale, medieval artists. That high indifference to the outward, that impassivity, has already a touch of the corpse in it: we see already Angelico* and the *Master of the Passion** in the artistic future. The suppression of the sensuous, the shutting of the door upon it, the ascetic interest, may be even now foreseen. Those abstracted gods, 'ready to melt out their essence fine into the winds,'* who can fold up their flesh as a garment, and still remain themselves, seem already to feel that bleak air, in which, like Helen of Troy, they wander as the spectres of the middle age.

Gradually, as the world came into the church, an artistic interest, native in the human soul, reasserted its claims. But Christian art was still dependent on pagan examples, building the shafts of pagan temples into its churches, perpetuating the form of the *basilica*, in later times, working the disused amphitheatres as stone-quarries. The sensuous expression of ideas which unreservedly discredit the world of sense, was the delicate problem which Christian art had before it. If we think of medieval painting, as it ranges from the early German schools, still with something of the air of the charnel-house about them, to the clear loveliness of Perugino,* we shall see how that problem was solved. In the very 'worship of sorrow'* the native blitheness of art asserted itself. The religious spirit, as Hegel says,* 'smiled through its tears.' So perfectly did the young Raphael infuse that

Heiterkeit, that pagan blitheness, into religious works, that his picture of Saint Agatha at Bologna became to Goethe a step in the evolution of *Iphigenie*[1]. But in proportion as the gift of smiling was found once more, there came also an aspiration towards that lost antique art, some relics of which Christian art had buried in itself, ready to work wonders when their day came.

The history of art has suffered as much as any history by trenchant and absolute divisions. Pagan and Christian art are sometimes harshly opposed, and the Renaissance is represented as a fashion which set in at a definite period. That is the superficial view: the deeper view is that which preserves the identity of European culture. The two are really continuous; and there is a sense in which it may be said that the Renaissance was an uninterrupted effort of the middle age, that it was ever taking place. When the actual relics of the antique were restored to the world, in the view of the Christian ascetic it was as if an ancient plague-pit had been opened. All the world took the contagion of the life of nature and of the senses. And now it was seen that the medieval spirit too had done something for the new fortunes of the antique. By hastening the decline of art, by withdrawing interest from it and yet keeping unbroken the thread of its traditions, it had suffered the human mind to repose itself, that when day came it might awake, with eyes refreshed, to those ancient, ideal forms.

The aim of a right criticism is to place Winckelmann in an intellectual perspective, of which Goethe is the foreground. For, after all, he is infinitely less than Goethe; and it is chiefly because at certain points he comes in contact with Goethe, that criticism entertains consideration of him. His relation to modern culture is a peculiar one. He is not of the modern world; nor is he wholly of the eighteenth century, although so much of his outer life is characteristic of it. But that note of revolt against the eighteenth century, which we detect in Goethe, was struck by Winckelmann. Goethe illustrates a union of the Romantic spirit, in its adventure, its

---

[1] *Italiänische Reise. Bologna*, 19 *Oct.* 1776.

variety, its profound subjectivity of soul, with Hellenism, in its transparency, its rationality, its desire of beauty—that marriage of Faust and Helena, of which the art of the nineteenth century is the child, the beautiful lad Euphorion, as Goethe conceives him, on the crags, in the 'splendour of battle and in harness as for victory,' his brows bound with light[1]. Goethe illustrates, too, the preponderance in this marriage of the Hellenic element; and that element, in its true essence, was made known to him by Winckelmann.

Breadth, centrality, with blitheness and repose, are the marks of Hellenic culture. Is such culture a lost art? The local, accidental colouring of its own age has passed from it; and the greatness that is dead looks greater when every link with what is slight and vulgar has been severed. We can only see it at all in the reflected, refined light which a great education creates for us. Can we bring down that ideal into the gaudy, perplexed light of modern life?

Certainly, for us of the modern world, with its conflicting claims, its entangled interests, distracted by so many sorrows, with many preoccupations, so bewildering an experience, the problem of unity with ourselves, in blitheness and repose, is far harder than it was for the Greek within the simple terms of antique life. Yet, not less than ever, the intellect demands completeness, centrality. It is this which Winckelmann imprints on the imagination of Goethe, at the beginning of life, in its original and simplest form, as in a fragment of Greek art itself, stranded on that littered, indeterminate shore of Germany in the eighteenth century. In Winckelmann, this type comes to him, not as in a book or a theory, but more importunately, because in a passionate life, in a personality. For Goethe, possessing all modern interests, ready to be lost in the perplexed currents of modern thought, he defines, in clearest outline, the eternal problem of culture—balance, unity with one's self, consummate Greek modelling.

It could no longer be solved, as in Phryne* ascending naked out of the water, by perfection of bodily form, or any

---

[1] *Faust, Th. ii. Act.* 3.

joyful union with the external world: the shadows had grown too long, the light too solemn, for that. It could hardly be solved, as in Pericles or Pheidias, by the direct exercise of any single talent: amid the manifold claims of our modern intellectual life, that could only have ended in a thin, one-sided growth. Goethe's Hellenism was of another order, the *Allgemeinheit* and *Heiterkeit*, the completeness and serenity, of a watchful, exigent intellectualism. *Im Ganzen, Guten, Wahren, resolut zu leben:**—is Goethe's description of his own higher life; and what is meant by life in the whole—*im Ganzen?* It means the life of one for whom, over and over again, what was once precious has become indifferent. Every one who aims at the life of culture is met by many forms of it, arising out of the intense, laborious, one-sided development of some special talent. They are the brightest enthusiasms the world has to show: and it is not their part to weigh the claims which this or that alien form of genius makes upon them. But the proper instinct of self-culture cares not so much to reap all that those various forms of genius can give, as to find in them its own strength. The demand of the intellect is to feel itself alive. It must see into the laws, the operation, the intellectual reward of every divided form of culture; but only that it may measure the relation between itself and them. It struggles with those forms till its secret is won from each, and then lets each fall back into its place, in the supreme, artistic view of life. With a kind of passionate coldness, such natures rejoice to be away from and past their former selves, and above all, they are jealous of that abandonment to one special gift which really limits their capabilities. It would have been easy for Goethe, with the gift of a sensuous nature, to let it overgrow him. It comes easily and naturally, perhaps, to certain 'other-worldly' natures to be even as the *Schöne Seele,** that ideal of gentle pietism, in *Wilhelm Meister:* but to the large vision of Goethe, this seemed to be a phase of life that a man might feel all round, and leave behind him. Again, it is easy to indulge the commonplace metaphysical instinct. But a taste for metaphysics may be one of those things which we must renounce, if we mean to mould our lives to artistic perfection. Philosophy serves culture, not by the fancied gift of absolute or transcendental knowledge, but by suggesting questions which help one to detect the passion, and strangeness, and dramatic contrasts of life.

But Goethe's culture did not remain 'behind the veil':* it ever emerged in the practical functions of art, in actual production. For him the problem came to be:—Can the blitheness and universality of the antique ideal be communicated to artistic productions, which shall contain the fulness of the experience of the modern world? We have seen that the development of the various forms of art has corresponded to the development of the thoughts of man concerning humanity, to the growing revelation of the mind to itself. Sculpture corresponds to the unperplexed, emphatic outlines of Hellenic humanism; painting to the mystic depth and intricacy of the middle age; music and poetry have their fortune in the modern world.

Let us understand by poetry all literary production which attains the power of giving pleasure by its form, as distinct from its matter. Only in this varied literary form can art command that width, variety, delicacy of resources, which will enable it to deal with the conditions of modern life. What modern art has to do in the service of culture is so to rearrange the details of modern life, so to reflect it, that it may satisfy the spirit. And what does the spirit need in the face of modern life? The sense of freedom. That naïve, rough sense of freedom, which supposes man's will to be limited, if at all, only by a will stronger than his, he can never have again. The attempt to represent it in art would have so little verisimilitude that it would be flat and uninteresting. The chief factor in the thoughts of the modern mind concerning itself is the intricacy, the universality of natural law, even in the moral order. For us, necessity is not, as of old, a sort of mythological personage without us, with whom we can do warfare. It is rather a magic web woven through and through us, like that magnetic system of which modern science speaks, penetrating us with a network, subtler than our subtlest nerves, yet bearing in it the central forces of the world. Can art represent men and women in these bewildering toils so as to give the spirit at least an equivalent for the sense of freedom? Certainly, in Goethe's romances, and even more in the romances of Victor Hugo, we have high examples of modern art dealing thus with modern life, regarding that life as the modern mind must regard it, yet reflecting upon it blitheness and repose. Natural laws we shall never modify, embarrass us as they may; but there is still something in the nobler or less noble attitude with which we watch their fatal combinations. In those romances of Goethe and Victor Hugo, in some excellent work done *after* them, this entanglement, this network of law, becomes the tragic situation, in which certain groups of noble men and women work out for themselves a supreme *dénouement*. Who, if he saw through all, would fret against the chain of circumstance which endows one at the end with those great experiences?

1867.

CONCLUSION[1]

*Λέγει που ‘Ηράκλειτος ὅτι πάντα χωρεῖ καὶ οὐδὲν μένει**

To regard all things and principles of things as inconstant modes of fashions has more and more become the tendency of modern thought. Let us begin with that which is without—our physical life. Fix upon it in one of its more exquisite intervals, the moment, for instance, of delicious recoil from the flood of water in summer heat. What is the whole physical life in that moment but a combination of natural elements to which science gives their names? But those elements, phosphorus and lime and delicate fibres, are present not in the human body alone: we detect them in places most remote from it. Our physical life is a perpetual motion of them—the passage of the blood, the waste and repairing of the lenses of the eye, the modification of the tissues of the brain under every ray of light and sound—processes which science reduces to simpler and more elementary forces. Like the elements of which we are composed, the action of these forces extends beyond us: it rusts iron and ripens corn. Far out on every side of us those elements are broadcast, driven in many currents; and birth and gesture and death and the springing of violets from the grave are but a few out of ten thousand resultant combinations. That clear, perpetual outline of face and limb is but an image of ours, under which we group them—a design in a web, the actual threads of which pass out beyond it. This at least of flame-like our life has, that it is but the concurrence, renewed from moment to moment, of forces parting sooner or later on their ways.

---

[1] This brief 'Conclusion' was omitted in the second edition of this book, as I conceived it might possibly mislead some of those young men into whose hands it might fall. On the whole, I have thought it best to reprint it here, with some slight changes which bring it closer to my original meaning. I have dealt more fully in *Marius the Epicurean* with the thoughts suggested by it.

Or if we begin with the inward world of thought and feeling, the whirlpool is still more rapid, the flame more eager and devouring. There it is no longer the gradual darkening of the eye, the gradual fading of colour from the wall—movements of the shore-side, where the water flows down indeed, though in apparent rest—but the race of the mid-stream, a drift of momentary acts of sight and passion and thought. At first sight experience seems to bury us under a flood of external objects, pressing upon us with a sharp and importunate reality, calling us out of ourselves in a thousand forms of action. But when reflexion begins to play upon those objects they are dissipated under its influence; the cohesive force seems suspended like some trick of magic; each object is loosed into a group of impressions—colour, odour, texture—in the mind of the observer. And if we continue to dwell in thought on this world, not of objects in the solidity with which language invests them, but of impressions, unstable, flickering, inconsistent, which burn and are extinguished with our consciousness of them, it contracts still further: the whole scope of observation is dwarfed into the narrow chamber of the individual mind. Experience, already reduced to a group of impressions, is ringed round for each one of us by that thick wall of personality through which no real voice has ever pierced on its way to us, or from us to that which we can only conjecture to be without. Every one of those impressions is the impression of the individual in his isolation, each mind keeping as a solitary prisoner its own dream of a world. Analysis goes a step further still, and assures us that those impressions of the individual mind to which, for each one of us, experience dwindles down, are in perpetual flight; that each of them is limited by time, and that as time is infinitely divisible, each of them is infinitely divisible also; all that is actual in it being a single moment, gone while we try to apprehend it, of which it may ever be more truly said that it has ceased to be than that it is. To such a tremulous wisp constantly re-forming itself on the stream, to a single sharp impression, with a sense in it, a relic more or less fleeting, of such moments gone by, what is real in our life fines itself down. It is with this movement, with the passage and dissolution of impressions, images, sensations, that analysis leaves off—that continual vanishing away, that strange, perpetual, weaving and unweaving of ourselves.

Philosophiren, says Novalis,* *ist dephlegmatisiren, vivificiren.* The service of philosophy, of speculative culture, towards the human spirit, is to rouse, to startle it to a life of constant and eager observation. Every moment some form grows perfect in hand or face; some tone on the hills or the sea is choicer than the rest; some mood of passion or insight or intellectual excitement is irresistibly real and attractive to us,—for that moment only. Not the fruit of experience, but experience itself, is the end. A counted number of pulses only is given to us of a variegated, dramatic life. How may we see in them all that is to be seen in them by the finest senses? How shall we pass most swiftly from point to point, and be present always at the focus where the greatest number of vital forces unite in their purest energy?

To burn always with this hard, gem-like flame, to maintain this ecstasy, is success in life. In a sense it might even be said that our failure is to form habits: for, after all, habit is relative to a stereotyped world, and meantime it is only the roughness of the eye that makes any two persons, things, situations, seem alike. While all melts under our feet, we may well grasp at any exquisite passion, or any contribution to knowledge that seems by a lifted horizon to set the spirit free for a moment, or any stirring of the senses, strange dyes, strange colours, and curious odours, or work of the artist's hands, or the face of one's friend. Not to discriminate every moment some passionate attitude in those about us, and in the very brilliancy of their gifts some tragic dividing of forces on their ways, is, on this short day of frost and sun, to sleep before evening. With this sense of the splendour of our experience and of its awful brevity, gathering all we are into one desperate effort to see and touch, we shall hardly have time to make theories about the things we see and touch. What we have to do is to be for ever curiously testing new opinions and courting new impressions, never acquiescing in a facile orthodoxy, of Comte,* or of Hegel, or of our own.

Philosophical theories or ideas, as points of view, instruments of criticism, may help us to gather up what might otherwise pass unregarded by us. 'Philosophy is the microscope of thought.'* The theory or idea or system which requires of us the sacrifice of any part of this experience, in consideration of some interest into which we cannot enter, or some abstract theory we have not identified with ourselves, or of what is only conventional, has no real claim upon us.

One of the most beautiful passages of Rousseau is that in the sixth book of the *Confessions*,* where he describes the awakening in him of the literary sense. An undefinable taint of death had clung always about him, and now in early manhood he believed himself smitten by mortal disease. He asked himself how he might make as much as possible of the interval that remained; and he was not biassed by anything in his previous life when he decided that it must be by intellectual excitement, which he found just then in the clear, fresh writings of Voltaire. Well! we are all *condamnés*,* as Victor Hugo says: we are all under sentence of death but with a sort of indefinite reprieve—*les hommes sont tous condamnés à mort avec des sursis indéfinis*: we have an interval, and then our place knows us no more. Some spend this interval in listlessness, some in high passions, the wisest, at least among 'the children of this world,'* in art and song. For our one chance lies in expanding that interval, in getting as many pulsations as possible into the given time. Great passions may give us this quickened sense of life, ecstasy and sorrow of love, the various forms of enthusiastic activity, disinterested or otherwise, which come naturally to many of us. Only be sure it is passion—that it does yield you this fruit of a quickened, multiplied consciousness. Of such wisdom, the poetic passion, the desire of beauty, the love of art for its own sake, has most. For art comes to you proposing frankly to give nothing but the highest quality to your moments as they pass, and simply for those moments' sake.

1868.

THE END

APPENDIX

DIAPHANEITÈ

THERE are some unworldly types of character which the world is able to estimate. It recognises certain moral types, or categories, and regards whatever falls within them as having a right to exist. The saint, the artist, even the speculative thinker, out of the world's order as they are, yet work, so far as they work at all, in and by means of the main current of the world's energy. Often it gives them late, or scanty, or mistaken acknowledgment; still it has room for them in its scheme of life, a place made ready for them in its affections. It is also patient of doctrinaires of every degree of littleness. As if dimly conscious of some great sickness and weariness of heart in itself, it turns readily to those who theorise about its unsoundness. To constitute one of these categories, or types, a breadth and generality of character is required. There is another type of character, which is not broad and general, rare, precious above all to the artist, a character which seems to have been the supreme moral charm in the Beatrice of the Commedia. It does not take the eye by breadth of colour; rather it is that fine edge of light, where the elements of our moral nature refine themselves to the burning point. It crosses rather than follows the main current of the world's life. The world has no sense fine enough for those evanescent shades, which fill up the blanks between contrasted types of character—delicate provision in the organisation of the moral world for the transmission to every part of it of the life quickened at single points! For this nature there is no place ready in its affections. This colourless, unclassified purity of life it can neither use for its service, nor contemplate as an ideal.

'Sibi unitus et simplificatus esse,' that is the long struggle of the Imitatio Christi. The spirit which it forms is the very opposite of that which regards life as a game of skill, and values things and persons as marks or counters of something to be gained, or achieved, beyond them. It seeks to value everything at its eternal worth, not adding to it, or taking from it, the amount of influence it may have for or against its own special scheme of life. It is the spirit that sees external circumstances as they are, its own power and tendencies as they are, and realises the given conditions of its life, not disquieted by the desire for change, or the preference of one part in life rather than another, or passion, or opinion. The character we mean to indicate achieves this perfect life by a happy gift of nature, without any struggle at all. Not the saint only, the artist also, and the speculative thinker, confused, jarred, disintegrated in the world, as sometimes they inevitably are, aspire for this simplicity to the last. The struggle of this aspiration with a lower practical aim in the mind of Savonarola has been subtly traced by the author of Romola. As language, expression, is the function of intellect, as art, the supreme expression, is the highest product of intellect, so this desire for simplicity is a kind of indirect self-assertion of the intellectual part of such natures. Simplicity in purpose and act is a kind of determinate expression in dexterous outline of one's personality. It is a kind of moral expressiveness; there is an intellectual triumph implied in it. Such a simplicity is characteristic of the repose of perfect intellectual culture. The artist and he who has treated life in the spirit of art desires only to be shown to the world as he really is; as he comes nearer and nearer to perfection, the veil of an outer life not simply expressive of the inward becomes thinner and thinner. This intellectual throne is rarely won. Like the religious life, it is a paradox in the world, denying the first conditions of man's ordinary existence, cutting obliquely the spontaneous order of things. But the character we have before us is a kind of prophecy of this repose and simplicity, coming as it were in the order of grace, not of nature, by some happy gift, or accident of birth or constitution, showing that it is indeed within the limits of man's destiny. Like all the higher forms of inward life this character is a subtle blending and interpenetration of intellectual, moral and spiritual elements. But it is as a phase of intellect, of culture, that it is most striking and forcible. It is a mind of taste lighted up by some spiritual ray within. What is meant by taste is an imperfect intellectual state; it is but a sterile kind of culture. It is the mental attitude, the intellectual manner of perfect culture, assumed by a happy instinct. Its beautiful way of handling everything that appeals to the senses and the intellect is really directed by the laws of the higher intellectual life, but while culture is able to trace those laws, mere taste is unaware of them. In the character before us, taste, without ceasing to be instructive, is far more than a mental attitude or manner. A magnificent intellectual force is latent within it. It is like the reminiscence of a forgotten culture that once adorned the mind; as if the mind of one φιλοσοφήσας ποτε μετ᾽ ἔρωτος, fallen into a new cycle, were beginning its spiritual progress over again, but with a certain power of anticipating its stages. It has the freshness without the shallowness of taste, the range and seriousness of culture without its strain and over-consciousness. Such a habit may be described as wistfulness of mind, the feeling that there is 'so much to know,' rather as a longing after what is unattainable, than as a hope to apprehend. Its ethical result is an intellectual guilelessness, or integrity, that instinctively prefers what is direct and clear, lest one's own confusion and intransparency should hinder the transmission from without of light that is not yet inward. He who is ever looking for the breaking of a light he knows not whence about him, notes with a strange heedfulness the faintest paleness in the sky. That truthfulness of temper, that receptivity, which professors often strive in vain to form, is engendered here less by wisdom than by innocence. Such a character is like a relic from the classical age, laid open by accident to our alien modern atmosphere. It has something of the clear ring, the eternal outline of the antique. Perhaps it is nearly always found with a corresponding outward semblance. The veil or mask of such a nature would be the very opposite of the 'dim blackguardism' of Danton, the type Carlyle has made too popular for the true interest of art. It is just this sort of entire transparency of nature that lets through unconsciously all that is really lifegiving in the established order of things; it detects without difficulty all sorts of affinities between its own elements, and the nobler elements in that order. But then its wistfulness and a confidence in perfection it has makes it love the lords of change. What makes revolutionists is either self-pity, or indignation for the sake of others, or a sympathetic perception of the dominant undercurrent of progress in things. The nature before us is revolutionist from the direct sense of personal worth, that χλιδή, that of pride of life, which to the Greek was a heavenly grace. How can he value what comes of accident, or usage, or convention, whose individual life nature itself has isolated and perfected? Revolution is often impious. They who prosecute revolution have to violate again and again the instinct of reverence. That is inevitable, since after all progress is a kind of violence. But in this nature revolutionism is softened, harmonised, subdued as by distance. It is the revolutionism of one who has slept a hundred years. Most of us are neutralised by the play of circumstances. To most of us only one chance is given in the life of the spirit and the intellect, and circumstances prevent our dexterously seizing that one chance. The one happy spot in our nature has no room to burst into life. Our collective life, pressing equally on every part of every one of us, reduces nearly all of us to the level of a colourless uninteresting existence. Others are neutralised, not by suppression of gifts, but by just equipoise among them. In these no single gift, or virtue, or idea, has an unmusical predominance. The world easily confounds these two conditions. It sees in the character before us only indifferentism. Doubtless the chief vein of the life of humanity could hardly pass through it. Not by it could the progress of the world be achieved. It is not the guise of Luther or Spinoza; rather it is that of Raphael, who in the midst of the Reformation and the Renaissance, himself lighted up by them, yielded himself to neither, but stood still to live upon himself, even in outward form a youth, almost an infant, yet surprising all the world. The beauty of the Greek statues was a sexless beauty; the statues of the gods had the least traces of sex. Here there is a moral sexlessness, a kind of impotence, an ineffectual wholeness of nature, yet with a divine beauty and significance of its own.

Over and over again the world has been surprised by the

heroism, the insight, the passion, of this clear crystal nature. Poetry and poetical history have dreamed of a crisis, where it must needs be that some human victim be sent down into the grave. These are they whom in its profound emotion humanity might choose to send. 'What,' says Carlyle, of Charlotte Corday, 'What if she had emerged from her secluded stillness, suddenly like a star; cruel-lovely, with half-angelic, half-dæmonic splendour; to gleam for a moment, and in a moment be extinguished; to be held in memory, so bright complete was she, through long centuries!'

Often the presence of this nature is felt like a sweet aroma in early manhood. Afterwards, as the adulterated atmosphere of the world assimilates us to itself, the savour of it faints away. Perhaps there are flushes of it in all of us; recurring moments of it in every period of life. Certainly this is so with every man of genius. It is a thread of pure white light that one might disentwine from the tumultuary richness of Goethe's nature. It is a natural prophecy of what the next generation will appear, renerved, modified by the ideas of this. There is a violence, an impossibility about men who have ideas, which makes one suspect that they could never be the type of any widespread life. Society could not be conformed to their image but by an unlovely straining from its true order. Well, in this nature the idea appears softened, harmonised as by distance, with an engaging naturalness, without the noise of axe or hammer.

People have often tried to find a type of life that might serve as a basement type. The philosopher, the saint, the artist, neither of them can be this type; the order of nature itself makes them exceptional. It cannot be the pedant, or the conservative, or anything rash and irreverent. Also the type must be one discontented with society as it is. The nature here indicated alone is worthy to be this type. A majority of such would be the regeneration of the world.

July, 1864.

EXPLANATORY NOTES

Dedication: C. L. S. was Charles Lancelot Shadwell (1840–1919), Fellow and the Provost of Oriel College, Oxford. One of the closest friends of Pater's adult life, Shadwell was Pater's private pupil as an undergraduate at Oxford, and his companion on Pater's first trip to Italy in 1865.

Epigraph: 'Though ye have lain among the pots, yet shall ye be as the wings of a dove covered with silver, and her feathers with yellow gold', Psalms 68:13.

PREFACE

xxix *'To see the object as in itself it really is'*: originally from Matthew Arnold's 'On Translating Homer' (1862) and repeated in the opening paragraph of Arnold's 'The Function of Criticism at the Present Time' (1864).

xxx *De se borner* ...: the quotation is by—not about—the French critic Charles Augustin Sainte-Beuve (1804–69), from a review of du Bellay's works in Sainte-Beuve's *Journal des Savants* of June 1867. Defining the *humanistes* at the time when the great works of Renaissance learning were first being published, making the work of the ancients available for the first time in printed books, Sainte-Beuve describes them as 'confining themselves to knowing beautiful things intimately, and nourishing themselves on these things as exquisitely discriminating amateurs, as accomplished humanists'.

xxxiii *the age of Pericles*: the great fifth century BC Athenian statesman whose period of prominence—approximately 460–429 BC—came to be known as the Age of Pericles.

xxxiii *Lorenzo*: Lorenzo il Magnifico (1449–92), head of the Florentine Republic during the 'Golden Age' of Florence.

TWO EARLY FRENCH STORIES

1 *Boccaccio*: Giovanni Boccaccio (1313–75), Italian author of the *Decameron*, a hundred stories published in 1353.

1 *how Dante himself expressly connects* . . .: see Dante's *Purgatorio* XI, 79–81.

2 *Jean Cousin and Germain Pilon*: Jean Cousin the elder (*c.*1490–1560) was a painter, engraver, and designer of stained glass. His son Jean to whom Pater may have been referring here was a glass-painter and book illustrator. Germain Pilon (1537–90) was a French sculptor of aristocratic figures, indebted to the school of Michelangelo.

the legend of Abelard: Abelard (1079–1142) fell in love with Heloïse (1101–1165) while working as her tutor in her uncle's house. They had a child and were secretly married; Heloïse was then sent to a convent and her uncle took revenge on Abelard by castrating him. This had happened by about 1118, by which time Abelard had become a monk and Heloïse a nun. Abelard continued to be a controversial teacher and was convicted of heresy by the Council of Sens and the Pope in 1140. He was eventually persuaded to submit to the council's verdict while on his way to Rome to defend himself.

3 *M. de Rémusat*: Charles François Marie, Comte de Rémusat (1797–1875), whose book *Abélard* Pater is quoting from here. *Trouvères* were troubadours.

Michelet: the French historian Jules Michelet (1798–1874), whose *Histoire de France*, vol. VII, Pater translates from here. Pater's view of the Renaissance is considerably influenced by this volume of Michelet's *Histoire* published in 1855.

Arnold of Brescia: (d.1155), powerful critic of the corruption of the clergy and papal power, he was eventually anathematized by the Pope in 1148, and condemned to death by the Emperor Frederick I.

4 *fair Rosamond*: Godstow nunnery in Oxfordshire was the retreat of 'fair Rosamond' Clifford courted by Henry II. She died and was buried there probably in 1176.

5 *après l'invention* . . .: Pater quotes and translates here from the French poet du Bellay's Preface to *L'Olive*. The full sentence is: 'As for those people who will not welcome this kind of writing, which they call obscure because it is beyond their understanding, I leave them with those who, after the invention of wheat, still want to live on acorns.'

the pretty volumes . . .: Pater is referring here to *Nouvelles Françoises en Prose du XIII siècle*, ed. L. Moland and C. d'Héricault, Paris 1856. Pater selectively translates the stories he quotes.

6 *the Doppelgänger*: literally the double-goer, a double, in various forms, of a living person.

the Dioscuri: Castor and Pollux, the twin sons of Zeus, are the Dioscuri; they became the constellation Gemini after their death.

10 *the Tenson and the Aubade*: Fauriel (see note below) defines the *Tenson* as 'Dialogues in which two or more speakers maintain contrary opinions on a given thesis'. The *Aubade* is a dawn song of lovers.

Bernard de Ventadour and Pierre Vidal: Bernard de Ventadour (1150–95) and Pierre Vidal (1175–1215) were famous troubadours.

M. Fauriel: Claude Charles Fauriel (1772–1844) was Professor of foreign literature at the Sorbonne, and author of *Histoire de la poésie provençale* (1846).

12 *cortois . . . et bien assis*: courtly . . . and well done.

15 '*Lord of terrible aspect*': see Dante's *Vita Nuova*, section 111.

16 *Notre-Dame de Paris*: published in 1834, by the great French writer Victor Hugo (1802–85).

the Albigensian movement: the Counts of Toulouse were famous for having given protection to the Albigensian heretics as well as supporting the troubadours.

Joachim of Flora: Joachim (*c.*1145–1202) was a renowned theologian and abbot of the monastery of San Giovanni in Fiore.

17 *the House Beautiful*: in *The Pilgrim's Progress* Bunyan writes of 'a very stately palace . . . the name whereof was beautiful' which was 'a house built for the relief and security of pilgrims' and later referred to as the 'House Beautiful'.

17–18 *the painter of the Last Supper*: Leonardo da Vinci.

18 *La vie . . .*: the life of the martyred saints Amis and Amile.

PICO DELLA MIRANDOLA

20 *Heine, in the Gods in Exile*: this essay by the German writer Heine (1797–1856) which Pater refers to throughout his writings, first appeared as 'Les Dieux en Exil' in the *Revue des deux mondes*, 1 April, 1853. Pater translates here, not from this version, but from Heine's revised German translation of the essay published in 1853–4.

22 *éclaircissement*: clarification.

23 *in recessu divinius aliquid*: more literally, 'some divine quality in the depths'.

   a 'madhouse-cell': Browning's two dramatic monologues, 'Porphyria's Lover' and 'Johannes Agricola in Meditation' appeared under the general title 'Madhouse Cells' in *Dramatic Lyrics* (1842).

   Marsilio Ficino: Italian philosopher and writer (1433–99).

24 *as M. Renan has pointed out*: Pater refers here to Renan's *Averroès et l'Averroisme* (1852).

27 *Savonarola's famous 'bonfire of vanities'*: in 1497 the Florentines were persuaded by Savonarola to burn their frivolous things, carnival masks, trivial books, obscene pictures, etc., in his famous bonfire. Girolamo Savonarola (1452–98), the Italian monk and martyr, was described as suffering 'burning indignation against the corruption of the church, and profoundest sorrow for the calamities of his country'.

32 *caesiis et vigilibus oculis*: 'his eyes grey and quick of look'.

   decenti rubore interspersa: 'intermingled with comely reds'.

SANDRO BOTTICELLI

33 *the gossip which Vasari accumulated*: see *Lives of the Artists*, bks. 1 and 2, by Giorgio Vasari (1511–74), the Italian painter and writer.

37 *the 'Desire of all nations'*: 'And I will shake all nations, and the Desire of all nations shall come: and I will fill this house with glory, saith the Lord of hosts', Haggai 2:7.

   enfants du choeur: children of the choir.

39 *Simonetta*: 'La bella Simonetta' Cattaneo, wife of Mario Vespucci and probably mistress of Giuliano de Medici (1453–78). She died young, in 1476, of consumption and her death was publicly mourned in Florence.

   Judith ... Justice ... Veritas: the pictures referred to are, respectively, *The Return of Judith*, *Fortitude*, and *The Calumny of Apelles*, all in the Uffizi, Florence.

LUCA DELLA ROBBIA

43 *Pheidias*: Pheidias (*c*.500–432 BC) organized Pericles' architectural schemes, including the sculptures for the Parthenon.

44 *the Venus of Melos*: the famous statue of the Venus de Milo in the Louvre, Paris, found on the island of Melos in 1820.

the wasting of that snow-image: see Vasari's *Lives*, bk. 2.

THE POETRY OF MICHELANGELO

47 *ex forti dulcedo*: 'De comedente exivit cibus, et de forti egressa est dulcedo': 'Out of the eater came forth meat, and out of the strong came forth sweetness', Judges 14:14.

48 *Grimm*: Pater is quoting here from *Leben Michelangelos* (1864) by Herman Friedrich Grimm.

51 *that unique presentment of Bacchus*: Michelangelo's marble statue the *Drunken Bacchus* in the Bargello in Florence. Pater writes again about this work in 'A Study of Dionysius' (1876) in *Greek Studies*.

52 *the great Matilda*: Matilda (*c*.1046–1115) was countess of Tuscany and Mistress of the Holy Roman Emperor Henry V.

par che amaro . . .: 'I seem to feel every sweetness as bitter', from Michelangelo's madrigal 'Amor, la morte a forza'. It seems that Pater knowingly used a spurious text here.

54 *un dolce amaro* . . .: 'a bitter sweet, a yes and no moves me'.

del suo prestino . . .: 'the shining light of its [the soul's] previous state'.

We know how Goethe . . .: a reference to Goethe's novel *Werther* (1774).

La vita del . . .: 'The life of my love is not my heart/The love by which I love you has no heart', from Sonnet XXVIII.

55 *chalybeate salt*: salt impregnated with iron.

56 *il bel del* . . .: 'the outward beauty that pleases the eye'.

trascenda . . .: 'going beyond to the universal form'.

la dove . . .: 'there where I first loved you'.

57 *the Oratory*: the Oratory of Divine Love was an aristocratic

societythat started in Rome, influenced by Lutheran ideas and aiming to reform the Catholic Church.

58 *Luca Signorelli*: prolific painter (*c*.1441–1523) famous for his fresco cycle in Orvieto cathedral.

Mino da Fiesole: Mino di Giovanni (*c*.1430–84) was a Florentine sculptor.

59 *Outre-tombe*: 'beside the grave'.

The young Cardinal Jacopo di Portogallo: the tomb was made by Antonio Rossellino (1427–79) between 1461 and 1466 for the church of S. Miniato al Monte near Florence. The epitaph reads 'I was distinguished for my comeliness and amazing modesty'.

the Pazzi conspirators: the Pazzi conspiracy of 1478 was an attempt to break the Medici's domination of Florence. Botticelli painted the conspirators hanging.

60 *a drawing of his at Oxford*: Pater is referring here to a black chalk Pietà done for Vittoria Colonna. It is now in Boston.

LEONARDO DA VINCI

63 *Homo minister* . . .: 'Man the minister and interpreter of nature', from Part II of Francis Bacon's *Instauratio Magna* (1620).

the Last Supper: Pater is referring here to the early deterioration of the *Last Supper*, and the consequent attempts to restore it.

64 *Carlo Amoretti*: a reference to Amoretti's *Memorie storiche su la vita gli studi e le opere di Leonardo da Vinci* (Milan, 1804).

Andrea del Verrocchio: Florentine painter, goldsmith, and sculptor (*c*.1435–88).

65–6 *Modesty and Vanity* . . . *Virgin of the Balances* . . . *Saint Anne*: *Modesty and Vanity*, now considered to be the work of Bernardino Luini, is in a private collection. The other two pictures are in the Louvre, though the *Virgin of the Balances* is no longer attributed to Leonardo.

67 *Vasari's story*: see Vasari's *Lives*, bk. 2.

68 *the well-ordered treatise*: the *Tratto della Pittura di Leonardo da Vinci*, with drawings by Poussin, was published in 1651.

Paracelsus or Cardan: Paracelsus was the pseudonym of the Swiss alchemist Theophrastus von Hohenheim (1493–1541). Geronimo Cardano (1501–76) was an Italian physician, astrologer, and mathematician.

69 *Ludovico Sforza*: (1451–1508) became Duke of Milan in 1494. His father Francesco Sforza (1401–66) was Duke of Milan from 1450 to his death.

the Duomo: the cathedral of Milan, at that time the largest church in the world.

70 *subtilitas naturae*: 'the subtlety of nature', see Bacon's *Novum Organum*, bk. 1, aphorism X.

72 *Quanto più . . .*: 'The more physical effort (or work) an art form involves, the more base it is.'

73 *bien-être*: well-being.

some of these drawings: none of the drawings mentioned in the next two paragraphs are by Leonardo. According to Kenneth Clark 'they are by Milanese pupils and reflect the idea of the Leonardesque'.

74 *Daughters of Herodias*: Salome, the daughter of Herodias, asked her father for the head of John the Baptist as a favour for her dancing. See Matthew 14:6–12, and Mark 6:17–29.

the head of a young man: in the Uffizi in Florence.

75 *Francesco Melzi*: Leonardo's friend and pupil (d.1570), to whom he left his drawings and papers.

Luini: Bernardino Luini (*c*.1485–1532), one of the most popular Milanese painters of the early sixteenth century.

76 *Théophile Gautier*: French writer (1811–72). Pater refers here to his essay 'Léonard de Vinci' in *Les dieux et les semidieux de la peinture* (1864).

Goethe's pensive sketch: Goethe's essay 'Giuseppe Bossi: über Leonardo da Vincis Abendmahl zu Mailand' (1817).

77 *the Brera*: the Brera Museum in Milan. The work referred to is no. 280 in the collection.

78 *Infelix sum*: 'I am unhappy.'

the 'triumph' of Cimabue: Giovanni Cimabue (1240–1302), the Florentine artist whose painting of the Virgin for the Rucellai chapel was celebrated by a procession carrying it from his house to the church.

80 *'the ends of the world are come'*: 'Now all these things happened unto them for ensamples: and they are written for our admoni-

tion, upon whom the ends of the world are come', 1 Corinthians
10:11.

81 *'fly before the storm'*: 'flee from storms' was the motto heading one
of Leonardo's manuscripts.

82 *Francis the First*: (1494–1547), king from 1515.

THE SCHOOL OF GIORGIONE

83 *the 'imaginative reason'*: the phrase is taken from Matthew
Arnold's essay, 'Pagan and Medieval Religious Sentiment'
(1864). The passage reads: 'The poetry of later paganism lived
by the senses and understanding; the poetry of medieval
Christianity lived by the heart and imagination. But the main
element of the modern spirit's life is neither the senses and
understanding, nor the heart and imagination; it is the imaginative reason.'

Lessing's . . . Laocoon: Gothold Ephraim Lessing (1729–81) published his treatise *Laocoon* in 1766.

85 *the Arena chapel*: at Padua.

86 *M. Alphonse Legros*: French artist (1837–1911) who lived in
London from 1863 and became professor of etching at the
Slade school.

87 *that song of Mariana's page: Measure for Measure*, IV. i.

90 *Giovanni Bellini*: Pater is referring here either to Gentile Bellini
(*c.*1429–1507) or Giovanni Bellini (1430/40–1516), both Venetian painters.

Browning's poem: 'Sordello', published in 1840. See bk. I, ll.
345–73, and bk. VI, ll. 828–35.

93 *the Concert*: it should be added now that it has been established
that the *Concert* is by Titian.

Catherine of Cornara, . . .: Catarina Cornaro (1454–1510) was
Queen of Cyprus until Venice took the island and forced her
abdication in 1489. She was given the castle and town of Asolo,
and held a brilliant court there.

Tuzio Costanzo: there is a portrait with the name of the sitter,
Mattheus Constantius, dated 1510, though he died in 1504. It is
thought by some to be by Giorgione.

says Vasari: see Vasari's *Lives*, bk. 2.

94 *Ridolfi*: Carlo Ridolfi in *Le Maraviglie dell'arte* (Padua, 1835).

95 *il fuoco Giorgionesco*: 'The Giorgionesque fire'.

96 *an ingenious passage of the Republic*: Plato's *Republic*, bk. 7.

Bandello's novels: Matteo Bandello (1480?–1562) whose *Novelle* were published in four volumes, 1554–73.

97 *the Fête Champêtre*: in the Louvre, now generally considered to be by Titian.

Jacob embraces Rachel . . .: this picture, in the Dresden gallery, is now considered to be by Palma Vecchio.

98 *the vraie vérité*: the important or genuine truth.

JOACHIM DU BELLAY

99 *Israël Silvestre*: (1621–91), designer and engraver to Louis XIV.

Maître Roux: Giovanni Battista Rosso Fiorentino (1494–1540).

Ronsard: Pierre de Ronsard (1524–85), French poet.

100 *the Clouets*: François Clouet (c.1510–72) and his father Jean Clouet (c.1485–1541) were both court painters.

Hemling: Hans Memling (1430/5–94), Bruges painter.

the Van Eycks: the brothers Hubert (d.1426) and Jan were founders of the Flemish school.

Villon: François Villon (1431–c.63), French poet.

Hours of Anne of Brittany: Anne of Brittany (1476–1514), wife of Charles VIII and Louis XII, whose illustrated and illuminated *Book of Hours* (c.1508) is one of the masterpieces of French miniature painting.

chansons de geste: Old French epic tales, told in verse.

the song of Roland: a reference to ll. 2249–51 of the most famous Old French epic, which in Scott-Moncrieff's translation run: 'Between his two arm-pits, upon his breast,/Crossways he folds those hands so white and fair,/Then mourns aloud, as was the custom there.' Folgoat is a small village near Brest.

Rabelais: François Rabelais (1494?–c.1553), French satirist whose most famous work was *Gargantua and Pantagruel* (1532–52).

101 *a Pindaric Ode*: reference to an ode, deriving from the Greek lyric poet Pindar (c.522–443 BC), which Pater goes on to explain.

101 *Avril, la grace* ...: Pater quotes here the sixth and seventh
    stanzas of the thirteen that compose the poem entitled 'Avril'
    from Belleau's 'La Première Jour de la bergerie'. The Andrew
    Lang translation, which Pater knew, is as follows: 'April, with
    thy gracious wiles,/Like the smiles,/Smiles of Venus; and thy
    breath/Like her breath, the God's delight/(From their height/
    They take the happy air beneath;)//It is thou that, of thy
    grace/From their place/In the far-off isles dost bring/Swallows
    over earth and sea,/Glad to be/Messengers of thee, and
    Spring.'

102 *the Pleiad*: the name is taken from the Pleiades, a cluster of a
    hundred stars, only six of which, in the constellation Taurus,
    can be seen with the naked eye.

    '*It is a remarkable fact* ...': from Sainte-Beuve's essay 'Anciens
    Poètes français: Joachim du Bellay', *Revue des deux mondes*,
    XXIV (15 October, 1840).

106 *The Queen of Scots* ...: Mary Stuart (1542–87) was brought up
    at the French court between 1548 and 1558. Catherine de
    Medici (1519–89) was wife to Henry II of France who reigned
    from 1547 to 1559.

    Malherbe: François de Malherbe (1555–1628), French poet.

    the Romanticists: a generation of French poets of the first half of
    the nineteenth century that included Hugo, Musset, Vigny,
    and Lamartine.

108 *Goudimel*: Claude Goudimel (*c.*1514–72) was well known as a
    composer of chansons and for his setting of psalms.

    That '*Lord of terrible aspect*': Rossetti's translation of 'uno
    segnore pauruso aspetto', from Dante's *Vita Nuova*.

109 *Francis the First* ... *Henry the Third* ... *Henry the Fourth*: kings of
    France whose dates, respectively, are: 1515–47,
    1574–89, 1589–1610.

110 *D'amour, de grace* ...: the second of 115 sonnets in *L'Olive*. A
    rough prose translation would run as follows; 'With love, with
    grace, and with high valour were the divine fires surrounded;
    and the heavens clothed themselves in a precious mantle of
    burning rays of various colours; everything was filled with
    beauty, with happinesss, the sea tranquil and the wind filled
    with grace when she was born in these lowly places, she who
    has plundered the world of all honour. She took her colour
    from the blanching lily, her head-dress from gold, her two lips

from the rose, and from the sun her eyes blazing with light: the sky showering her with his wealth left, enclosed in her soul, his seeds, and her name took immortality from the gods.'

110 *Montaigne's Essays*: Michel de Montaigne (1533–92), French politician and writer whose essays were published in several books between 1580 and 1588.

Rousseau: Jean-Jacques Rousseau (1712–78), French writer and political philosopher. Pater's reference here is to Rousseau's *Confessions* (1770).

111 *the Grisons*: the mountainous and glaciated eastern cantons of Switzerland.

Ronsard's . . . one famous ode: no. XVII 'À Cassandre' in the first book of *Les Odes*.

112 *A vous . . .*: the song is one of the 'Jeux Rustiques'. Lang's translation is as follows:

> 'To you, troop so fleet,
> That with winged wandering feet,
> Through the wide world pass,
> And with soft murmuring
> Toss the green shades of spring
> In woods and grass,
> Lily and violet
> I give, and blossoms wet,
> Roses and dew;
> This branch of blushing roses,
> Whose fresh bud uncloses,
> Wind-flowers too.
> Ah, winnow with sweet breath,
> Winnow the holt and heath,
> Round this retreat;
> Where all the golden morn
> We fan the gold o' the corn,
> In the sun's heat.'

WINCKELMANN

114 *Et ego . . .*: 'I also have been in Arcadia', which in Virgil's *Eclogues* was an ideal land, the home of Pan, the shepherd's god.

114 *Goethe's fragments* ...: Pater refers here to Goethe's essay 'Winckelmann', first published in 1805.

115 *famulus*: an attendant to a scholar.

'*vowelled*' *Greek*: an allusion to Keat's *Lamia*, pt. 2, 1.200: 'While fluent Greek a vowel'd undersong/Kept up ...'.

'*He felt in himself* ...': from *De l'Allemagne* (1810) by Madame de Staël (1766–1817).

'*a house not made with hands*': 2 Corinthians 5:1.

116 *Homo vagus et inconstans*: 'a purposeless and inconstant man'.

Schiller: Johann Christoph Friedrich von Schiller (1759–1805), German poet, dramatist, and philosopher.

Voltaire: François Marie Arouet de Voltaire (1694–1778), French philosopher, historian, dramatist, and man of letters.

116 *Iphigenie*: Goethe's 'French Classical' play, completed in 1780.

117 *Christian Wolff*: (1679–1754), professor of mathematics and natural philosophy at the university of Halle.

Emmanuel Kant: (1724–1804), German philosopher.

the Lysis: one of Plato's minor dialogues on the subject of love and friendship.

118 *Oeser*: Adam Friedrich Oeser (1717–99), German painter and etcher.

Hermione melts ...: see Shakespeare's *The Winter's Tale*, V. iii.

119 '*You know* ...': from 'Essai sur la physiognomie' (1783) by Johann Caspar Lavater (1741–1801), French physiognomist, theologian, mystic, and poet.

'*A lowly childhood* ...': Pater translates again from Goethe's essay, 'Winckelmann'.

120 *the part of Maecenas*: Maecenas (c.74/64–8BC) was the patron of Virgil, Horace, Propertius, and Varrius among others.

121 *Savonarola*: see Pico della Miranda, note to p.27.

122 *Charlotte Corday*: (1768–93), murdered the revolutionary leader Marat in 1793, and was condemned by the revolutionary tribunal and guillotined.

the Phaedrus: one of the Platonic dialogues.

123 *Guido's archangel*: Winckelmann was referring to Guido Reni's painting 'Archangel Michael' in the Capuccini church in Rome.

124 *a passage in which ...*: in Quinet's 'Les Revolutions d'Italie', *Œuvres complètes* (Paris, 1857–70).

125 *Pheidias*: fifth century BC Greek sculptor and architect.

125 *palaestra*: place for the practice and teaching of wrestling and other sports.

127 *another fresco*: the 'Parnassus'.

Castalia: a spring on Mt. Parnassus sacred to the muses, and so a source of inspiration.

this other 'City of God': 'There is a river, the streams whereof shall make glad the city of God', Psalm 46:4.

the beautiful story of Herodotus: see Herodotus' *History*, bk. IV, ch. 78. Scyles, the Scythian king born of a Greek mother, came to prefer the culture of the Greeks to that of the Scythians. So he would go with his army to visit a particular Greek town, leave the army outside the city, and enter alone having changed into Greek clothes. Guard was kept to make sure no Scythian saw him in these clothes. He would sometimes stay for over a month. He did this repeatedly, eventually marrying a woman of the town, and building himself a house there.

128 *Olympian Zeus and the Athene Polias*: Pater is referring here to Phidias' enormous statues of Zeus at Olympia and the Athene Polias (Polias meaning 'guardian of the city') of the Parthenon in Athens.

'the classical polytheism ...': from 'An Essay on the Development of Christian Doctrine' (1845) by John Henry Newman (1801–90).

129 *'rise up with wings as eagles'*: 'But they that wait upon the Lord shall renew their strength: they shall mount up with wings as eagles; they shall run and not be weary; and they shall walk and not faint', Isaiah 40:31.

130 *the power of the wing*: an allusion to Plato's *Phaedrus* where the soul is likened to a wing.

Pausanias: Greek writer of the second half of the second century AD, author of a guide book on Greece, *Helladus Periegesis*. Pater refers here to bk. 2, pt. 4, sec. 5.

Athenaeus: (*c.*AD 200), author of a collection of fragments from nearly 800 writers entitled *Deipnosophistai*.

131 *addolorata*: Our Lady of Sorrows.

Chthonian divinities: the gods of the Underworld.

131 *Angelico*: Frate Giovanni da Fiesole (1387–1455).

tanquam lana ...: 'His head and his hair were white like wool, as white as snow; and his eyes were as a flame of fire', Revelation 1:14.

132 *Diana of Ephesus*: Diana (otherwise known as Artemis) of Ephesus was a primitive goddess of nature and fertility in ancient Ionia. She was represented as a figure with lots of breasts but wearing grave-clothes below the waist.

Venus of Melos: see Luca della Robbia, note to p. 44.

'*nimbly and sweetly recommending itself*': see Shakespeare's *Macbeth*, I. vi.i.

palaestra: see note to p. 125 above.

'*I take ...*': spoken by Kritobulos in Xenophon's *Symposium* (*c*.430–355 BC).

135 *a Memnon waiting for the day*: Memnon in Greek mythology was the son of Tithonus and Eos. There was a legend that the colossal statue near Egyptian Thebes was a statue of this Memnon; and that this statue emitted a musical sound when first touched by the rays of the morning sun. This was considered to be Memnon's greeting to his mother, the dawn. See Hegel's *Aesthetik*, 1, 449–50.

137 *Heiterkeit ... Allgemeinheit*: Pater takes these terms from Hegel's *Aesthetik*.

138 *Dramatis Personae*: (1864). The 'situation' of 'Le Byron de nos jours' is one in which a young, though now miserably married, young woman reproaches a famous old poet for not declaring his love for her ten years before, when there was an opportunity to do so.

139 *Apollo ...*: in the third Homeric hymn the story is told of Apollo killing a dragon in Pytho, taking the name Python and building a temple for commemoration. There is a statue, much admired by Winckelmann, of the Apollo Belvedere in the Vatican Museum, Rome.

Venus with the apple of Paris ...: in a competition among the goddesses Paris, son of Priam, King of Troy, awarded a golden apple to Aphrodite for offering him the most beautiful woman in the world as his wife.

Laocoon: famous sculpture (*c*.160–130 BC) in the Vatican museum of the Trojan priest of Apollo, Laocoon, and his two sons struggling with the sea-serpents that finally killed all three. The story is told in bk. 2 of the *Aeneid*.

140 *Panathenaic frieze*: the Parthenon frieze in Athens of the panathenaic procession (part of the yearly festival in honour of Athene, in Athens).

the adorante: the Hellenistic bronze statue called 'Boy Praying' in the Berlin Museum.

says Hegel: Pater translates here from Hegel's *Aesthetik*, bk. 2.

142 *Plato's false astronomer*: see bk. 2 of Plato's *Republic*.

I did but taste . . .: 1 Samuel 14:43.

143 *Theocritus*: Greek poet (*c*.270 BC), originator of pastoral poetry.

Victor Hugo's Travailleurs de la Mer . . . Les Misérables: published respectively, 1865 and 1862.

144 *Adonis*: the beautiful youth Aphrodite fell in love with and from whose blood, when he was killed by a boar when hunting, she created the anemone. The gods of the Underworld let Adonis spend half the year on earth with her to assuage her great grief.

Hyacinthus: a youth loved by Apollo and killed by a discus thrown by the god.

Demeter: Greek earth goddess and mother of Persephone who was abducted by Hades and taken to the underworld; after a great search Demeter recovered her daughter, but only for two-thirds of every year. She established the Eleusian mysteries to commemorate her trials.

Hyperion: the Titan, father of Helios, the sun.

Oceanus: the Titan, father of the river-gods and water-nymphs. The Olympian gods conquered and succeeded the Titans.

Angelico: see note to p. 131 above.

Master of the Passion: possibly the 'Master of the Berlin Passion', the engraver of the Lower Rhine.

'ready to melt . . .': from Keats's *Endymion*, bk. I, ll. 95–100.

Perugino: Pietro Vanucci (*c*.1450–1523), Italian artist born in Umbria, who did his most famous work in Rome, Florence, and Perugia.

'worship of sorrow': in Pater's revised 1878 version of his essay 'The Myth of Demeter and Persephone' he writes that: ' "the

worship of sorrow'', as Goethe called it . . . was not without its function in Greek religion'.

144 *as Hegel says*: see Hegel's *Aesthetik*, bk. 1.

146 *Phryne*: famous courtesan of the fourth century BC who bathed in the sea at the festival in Eleusis and became the model for 'Aphrodite Anadyomene' by the great painter of antiquity, Apelle.

147 *Im Ganzen* . . .: Pater follows Carlyle's misquotation of Goethe in his essay 'Schiller' (1831). Goethe actually wrote: 'Im Ganzen, Guten, Schönen/Resolut zu leben'—'In wholeness, good, beauty/Resolute to live'.

Schöne Seele: 'beautiful soul'.

148 *'behind the veil'*: possibly an allusion to Tennyson's 'In Memoriam' (1850), LV.

CONCLUSION

150 *Greek epigraph*: in Jowett's translation, 'Heraclitus says "All things are in motion and nothing at rest." ' In *Plato and Platonism* (1893) Pater translated this as 'All things give way: nothing remaineth.'

152 *Novalis*: the pseudonym of Baron Friedrich von Hardenberg (1772–1801), German writer; the quotation is from 'Fragmente 2', werke 3, 64 (Heidelberg, 1957).

Comte: Auguste Comte (1798–1857), French philosopher and originator of Positivism.

153 *'Philosophy is . . .'*: from Hugo's *Les Misérables*, pt. 5, vol. 1, bk. 2, ch. 2.

Confessions: (1770). It should be added that Rousseau does not mention reading Voltaire.

we are all condamnés: from Hugo's *Le Dernier Jour d'un condamné* (1832).

'the children of this world': 'And the Lord commended the unjust steward, because he had done wisely: for the children of this world are in their generation wiser than the children of light', Luke 16:8.